Python Networking 101

Navigating essentials of networking, socket programming, AsyncIO, python libraries, network testing, simulations and Ansible Automation

Odette Windsor

Published by: GitforGits
Publisher: Sonal Dhandre
www.gitforgits.com
support@gitforgits.com

Printed in India

First Printing: May 2023

ISBN: 978-8119177134

Cover Design by: Kitten Publishing

For permission to use material from this book, please contact GitforGits at support@gitforgits.com.

Content

Preface

"Python Networking 101" is the ultimate guide for aspiring network administrators looking to build their skills in network management and automation using Python. With a comprehensive and hands-on approach, this book covers the most important aspects of networking, including network fundamentals, network automation, monitoring, security, topology, and testing.

The book begins with an overview of the Python language and its libraries used for networking tasks. Each chapter then focuses on a specific networking task, providing readers with a deep understanding of the topic and practical demonstrations using Python libraries. By the end of each chapter, readers will be well-versed in the execution and implementation of these tasks. Throughout the book, readers will learn about the best Python libraries preferred by network administrators, including Netmiko, Paramiko, SNMP, Flask, AsyncIO, and more. Practical examples and exercises will help them gain hands-on experience in working with these libraries to achieve various networking objectives.

The book also discusses advanced network automation techniques, providing insights into network automation frameworks, such as Ansible, and how to build custom network automation solutions using Python. By the end of the book, readers will be equipped with the knowledge to integrate Python with network management tools, making them efficient and effective network administrators.

In this book you will learn how to:

- Master Python language and its networking libraries for network administration tasks.
- Monitor and analyze network performance and troubleshoot issues effectively.
- Enhance network security using Python libraries and best practices.
- Get well versed with with Netmiko, Paramiko, Socket, PySNMP, AsyncIO, and SimPy.
- Develop custom network services and interact with RESTful APIs using Python.
- Improve performance with asynchronous programming using AsyncIO in network applications.
- Get hands-on with Ansible to create playbooks and perform every possible network automation.
- Perform network testing, simulation, and analyze results for optimized performance.

- Manage and automate network configuration changes and ensure compliance.
- Leverage advanced network automation techniques and frameworks for efficient administration.

GitforGits

Prerequisites

"Python Networking 101" is designed to provide readers with the skills required to excel as a network administrator. The practical approach, coupled with real-world examples, ensures that readers can implement the techniques learned in their professional careers. Knowing Python and basics of computer networks is sufficient to begin with this book.

Codes Usage

Are you in need of some helpful code examples to assist you in your programming and documentation? Look no further! Our book offers a wealth of supplemental material, including code examples and exercises.

Not only is this book here to aid you in getting your job done, but you have our permission to use the example code in your programs and documentation. However, please note that if you are reproducing a significant portion of the code, we do require you to contact us for permission.

But don't worry, using several chunks of code from this book in your program or answering a question by citing our book and quoting example code does not require permission. But if you do choose to give credit, an attribution typically includes the title, author, publisher, and ISBN. For example, "Python Networking 101 by Odette Windsor".

If you are unsure whether your intended use of the code examples falls under fair use or the permissions outlined above, please do not hesitate to reach out to us at support@gitforgits.com.

We are happy to assist and clarify any concerns.

Acknowledgement

I owe a tremendous debt of gratitude to GitforGits, for their unflagging enthusiasm and wise counsel throughout the entire process of writing this book. Their knowledge and careful editing helped make sure the piece was useful for people of all reading levels and comprehension skills. In addition, I'd like to thank everyone involved in the publishing process for their efforts in making this book a reality. Their efforts, from copyediting to advertising, made the project what it is today.

Finally, I'd like to express my gratitude to everyone who has shown me unconditional love and encouragement throughout my life. Their support was crucial to the completion of this book. I appreciate your help with this endeavour and your continued interest in my career.

Prologue

In today's fast-paced digital world, networks are the backbone of every organization. They facilitate communication, collaboration, and the exchange of information, making it crucial for businesses to have skilled network administrators managing their networks. As a network administrator, you will be responsible for designing, implementing, and maintaining networks that keep organizations running smoothly.

The increasing complexity of networks and the demand for greater efficiency has led to the rapid growth of network automation. Network automation helps reduce manual intervention, minimize errors, and improve network performance. Python has emerged as a popular choice for network administrators due to its simplicity, readability, and wide range of libraries that cater to various networking tasks.

"Python Networking 101" is designed to help you embark on your journey to become a skilled network administrator. This book will guide you through the fundamentals of networking and Python, providing a solid foundation for you to build upon. Each chapter introduces a new networking task, explaining the concepts, demonstrating their implementation using Python libraries, and providing practical examples for you to practice. The book begins with an introduction to the Python language, networking concepts, and libraries commonly used in networking tasks. As you progress through the chapters, you will learn about socket programming, network automation, monitoring, security, and more. You will also explore advanced topics such as network topology, visualization, asynchronous programming, and network testing.

By the end of the book, you will have a thorough understanding of the role of a network administrator, the various networking tasks involved, and how to perform these tasks using Python. You will also be introduced to advanced network automation techniques and frameworks, equipping you with the knowledge to create custom network automation solutions and integrate Python with other network management tools.

The practical approach and real-world examples used in this book will ensure that you can apply the skills learned to your professional career. Whether you are a beginner looking to start your career in network administration or an experienced professional seeking to enhance your skills, "Python Networking 101" will serve as a valuable resource for your growth and development.

Chapter 1: Introduction to Python and Networking

Overview of Python Language

Python is a high-level, interpreted programming language that was created by Guido van Rossum and first released in 1991. Its simplicity, readability, and versatility have made it one of the most popular programming languages globally, with a wide range of applications, including web development, data analysis, artificial intelligence, and, of course, networking. Python's appeal as a programming language lies in its design philosophy, which emphasizes code readability and ease of use. The language features a clean, English-like syntax that allows developers to express their ideas concisely and efficiently. This has made Python an excellent choice for beginners and experienced developers alike, as it enables rapid development and prototyping without sacrificing performance.

One of the key strengths of Python is its extensive standard library, which offers built-in modules for various tasks, including file handling, regular expressions, and even basic networking. In addition to the standard library, Python boasts a thriving ecosystem of third-party libraries and frameworks that further extend its capabilities. This ecosystem is made possible by the Python Package Index (PyPI), a repository of over 200,000 packages that can be easily installed and used in your projects.

Python for Networking

In the context of networking, Python has emerged as a powerful tool for network administrators due to its ease of use and the availability of numerous libraries tailored for networking tasks. The language's simplicity allows network administrators to quickly write scripts and automate repetitive tasks, reducing the chances of human error and improving efficiency. Python's cross-platform compatibility means that the same script can be run on different operating systems with minimal modifications, making it a versatile choice for managing multi-platform networks.

Python's rise in popularity for networking operations can be attributed to several factors, including:

Readability and simplicity: Python's syntax is designed to be easily readable and understandable, making it ideal for writing clear and maintainable code. This is particularly important in networking tasks, where complex configurations and data manipulation can quickly become overwhelming.

Extensive libraries: Python offers a wide range of libraries that simplify networking tasks, such as Netmiko, Paramiko, and SNMP, among others. These libraries provide abstractions and utility functions that make it easy to work with various network protocols and devices without having to reinvent the wheel.

Community support: Python has a large and active community of developers and network professionals who contribute to the development of new libraries, share knowledge, and provide support through forums and online resources.

Cross-platform compatibility: Python runs on various platforms, including Windows, macOS, Linux, and Unix, making it an ideal choice for managing networks with diverse operating systems.

Scalability: Python can be used for small-scale scripting tasks as well as large-scale network automation projects. Its flexibility and adaptability make it a suitable choice for network administrators at any level of expertise.

In this chapter, we will explore the fundamentals of Python as a programming language, including its syntax and data structures. We will also introduce the most popular Python libraries used for networking tasks and guide you through the process of setting up your Python environment for network administration.

Setting up Python Environment

Setting up a Python environment on Windows is straightforward. Follow these step-by-step instructions to get started:

Download Python Installer

Visit the official Python website at:
https://www.python.org/downloads/release/python-3113/

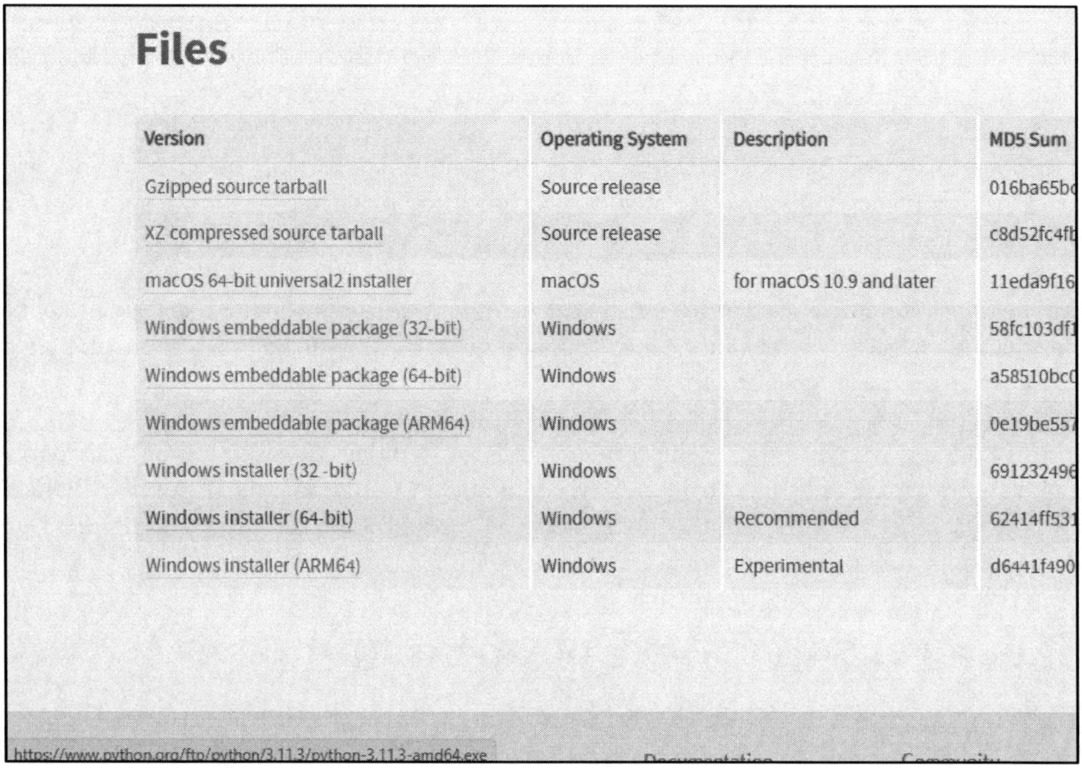

Files

Version	Operating System	Description	MD5 Sum
Gzipped source tarball	Source release		016ba65b...
XZ compressed source tarball	Source release		c8d52fc4f...
macOS 64-bit universal2 installer	macOS	for macOS 10.9 and later	11eda9f16...
Windows embeddable package (32-bit)	Windows		58fc103df...
Windows embeddable package (64-bit)	Windows		a58510bc0...
Windows embeddable package (ARM64)	Windows		0e19be55...
Windows installer (32 -bit)	Windows		691232496...
Windows installer (64-bit)	Windows	Recommended	62414ff53...
Windows installer (ARM64)	Windows	Experimental	d6441f490...

https://www.python.org/ftp/python/3.11.3/python-3.11.3-amd64.exe

On this page, you will find the latest Python release for Windows. Click on the download link for the "Windows x86-64 executable installer" if you have a 64-bit system, or "Windows x86 executable installer" if you have a 32-bit system.

Save the installer to your desired location on your computer.

Install Python

Navigate to the location where you saved the Python installer and double-click on the executable file to start the installation process.

In the installation window, you will see an option at the bottom that says "Add Python to PATH." It is recommended to check this box, as it will add Python to your system's PATH variable, making it easier to access Python from the command line.

Click on the "Install Now" button to begin the installation. The installer will copy the necessary files and set up Python on your system.

Verify the Installation

Once the installation is complete, open a new Command Prompt by pressing the Windows key, typing "cmd" in the search bar, and hitting Enter.

In the Command Prompt, type python --version and press Enter. You should see the Python version number displayed, indicating that Python has been installed successfully.

Install Code Editor

While it is possible to write Python code using a simple text editor like Notepad, using a dedicated code editor can significantly improve your productivity. Some popular code editors for Python development include Visual Studio Code, Sublime Text, and Atom. Download and install your preferred code editor.

Setup a Virtual Environment

Python allows you to create virtual environments that can isolate dependencies for each project. This is helpful when you work on multiple projects with different library requirements. Below is how to set up a virtual environment:

Open the Command Prompt.

Navigate to the directory where you want to create your project folder using the cd command.

For example, to navigate to the "Documents" folder, type cd Documents and press Enter.

Create a new project folder using the mkdir command, followed by the folder name. For example, to create a folder called "my_project," type mkdir my_project and press Enter.

Navigate to the newly created project folder using the cd command. For example, type cd my_project and press Enter.

Create a virtual environment in the project folder by typing python -m venv my_project_env and pressing Enter. Replace "my_project_env" with the desired name for your virtual environment.

Activate the virtual environment by typing my_project_env\Scripts\activate and pressing Enter. Your command prompt should now display the name of your virtual environment, indicating that it is active.

Now your Python environment is set up, and you are ready to start writing Python code for networking tasks.

Python Syntax and Data Structures

Python is known for its simple and clean syntax, which makes it easy to learn and understand. Let us refresh your knowledge of Python syntax and data structures in this overview.

Variables and Data Types

In Python, variables do not require explicit declaration, and their data types are inferred automatically based on the value assigned to them.

Python supports various data types, including:

- Integers (e.g., 42)
- Floating-point numbers (e.g., 3.14)
- Strings (e.g., "Hello, World!")
- Booleans (True or False)

Examples:

```
number = 42
pi = 3.14
message = "Hello, World!"
is_active = True
```

Arithmetic Operators

Python provides basic arithmetic operators for performing mathematical operations:

- Addition: +
- Subtraction: -
- Multiplication: *
- Division: /
- Floor Division: //
- Exponentiation: **
- Modulus: %

Examples:

```
addition = 3 + 5
subtraction = 10 - 2
multiplication = 4 * 6
division = 15 / 3
floor_division = 7 // 2
exponentiation = 2 ** 3
modulus = 10 % 3
```

String Formatting

Python offers several ways to format strings, including:

- String concatenation: +
- %-formatting
- str.format()
- f-strings (Python 3.6+)

Examples:

```
name = "John"
age = 30

# String concatenation
message = "My name is " + name + " and I am " + str(age) + " years old."

# %-formatting
message = "My name is %s and I am %d years old." % (name, age)

# str.format()
message = "My name is {} and I am {} years old.".format(name, age)

# f-strings
message = f"My name is {name} and I am {age} years old."
```

Conditionals

Python uses if, elif, and else statements for conditional execution:

```python
age = 18

if age < 13:
    print("You are a child.")
elif age < 18:
    print("You are a teenager.")
else:
    print("You are an adult.")
```

Loops

Python provides for and while loops for iteration:

- for loop: Used for iterating over a sequence (list, tuple, string, etc.)

```python
fruits = ["apple", "banana", "cherry"]

for fruit in fruits:
    print(fruit)
```

- while loop: Repeats a block of code as long as a condition is true.

```python
count = 0

while count < 5:
    print(count)
    count += 1
```

Functions

Functions in Python are defined using the def keyword and can accept arguments and return values:

```python
def greet(name):
    return f"Hello, {name}!"


message = greet("John")
print(message)  # Output: Hello, John!
```

Data Structures

Python provides several built-in data structures, including:

- Lists: Mutable, ordered collections of items.

```python
fruits = ["apple", "banana", "cherry"]

# Access items
print(fruits[0])  # Output: apple

# Modify items
fruits[1] = "blueberry"

#Add items
fruits.append("orange")

Remove items
fruits.remove("apple")

List comprehensions
squares = [x**2 for x in range(1, 6)]
```

- Tuples: Immutable, ordered collections of items.

```python
colors = ("red", "green", "blue")

# Access items
```

```python
print(colors[1])  # Output: green

# Tuples are immutable, so you cannot modify them directly
# However, you can create a new tuple with the desired modifications
```

- Sets: Unordered collections of unique items.

```python
unique_numbers = {1, 2, 3, 4, 4, 5}

# Add items
unique_numbers.add(6)

# Remove items
unique_numbers.remove(1)

# Set operations (union, intersection, difference)
a = {1, 2, 3}
b = {2, 3, 4}
union = a | b
intersection = a & b
difference = a - b
```

- Dictionaries: Collections of key-value pairs.

```python
person = {
    "name": "John",
    "age": 30,
    "city": "New York"
}

# Access items
print(person["name"])  # Output: John
```

```python
# Modify items
person["age"] = 31

# Add items
person["country"] = "USA"

# Remove items
del person["city"]

# Dictionary comprehensions
squares = {x: x**2 for x in range(1, 6)}
```

Exception Handling

Python uses try, except, finally, and raise statements to handle exceptions:

```python
def divide(a, b):
    try:
        result = a / b
    except ZeroDivisionError:
        print("Division by zero is not allowed.")
    else:
        print(f"The result is {result}.")
    finally:
        print("Finished executing the divide function.")


divide(10, 2)
divide(10, 0)
```

Modules and Packages

Modules in Python are simply files containing Python code. You can import a module using the import statement, and access its functions and variables using the dot notation:

```python
# my_module.py
```

```python
def greet(name):
    return f"Hello, {name}!"


# main.py
import my_module


message = my_module.greet("John")
print(message)
```

Packages are a way to organize related modules into a single directory. To create a package, simply create a directory and include an __init__.py file in it:

```
my_package/
    __init__.py
    my_module.py
```

Classes and Objects

Python supports object-oriented programming and allows you to create custom classes:

```python
class Dog:
    def __init__(self, name, age):
        self.name = name
        self.age = age

    def bark(self):
        print("Woof!")


my_dog = Dog("Buddy", 3)
print(my_dog.name)  # Output: Buddy
my_dog.bark()  # Output: Woof!
```

With this, you have refreshed the much needed essential aspects of Python syntax and data structures, including variables, data types, operators, conditionals, loops, functions, exception handling, modules, packages, and object-oriented programming. With this refresher, you should be well-prepared to tackle networking tasks using Python.

Essentials of Networking

Networking is the process of connecting multiple computing devices to share resources, information, and services. As a network administrator, you'll be responsible for setting up, maintaining, and troubleshooting networks. Let us dive into the essentials of networking to kickstart your journey towards becoming a network administrator.

Network Components

A computer network consists of several key components:

- Nodes: Individual devices connected to the network, such as computers, servers, routers, and switches.
- Communication media: Physical or wireless connections that transmit data between nodes, including Ethernet cables, fiber optics, and Wi-Fi signals.
- Networking hardware: Devices that facilitate network communication, such as routers, switches, and access points.
- Networking software: Applications and protocols that govern data transmission and network management.
- Network Types:

Networks can be classified based on their size, scope, and purpose:

1. Personal Area Network (PAN): A small network that connects devices within a user's personal workspace, typically over Bluetooth or Wi-Fi.
2. Local Area Network (LAN): A network that spans a limited area, such as a home, office, or campus. LANs typically use Ethernet or Wi-Fi to connect devices.
3. Wide Area Network (WAN): A network that spans a large geographical area, often connecting multiple LANs. The Internet is an example of a WAN.
4. Virtual Private Network (VPN): A secure, encrypted network that extends over the public Internet, allowing remote users to access a private network as if they were physically connected.

Network Topologies

Network topologies play a crucial role in determining the efficiency, reliability, and scalability of a network. Understanding these topologies allows network administrators to design and optimize networks to meet specific requirements.

Common network topologies include:

1) Bus: Bus topology is an economical choice for small networks, as it requires less cable compared to other topologies. However, it is less reliable because if the central cable fails, the entire network is affected. Additionally, data collisions can occur due to the shared communication medium, reducing performance as the network grows.

2) Star: Star topology is widely used in modern networks, as the central hub or switch acts as a single point of control, simplifying network management. It offers better reliability compared to bus topology, as the failure of one node does not impact the entire network. However, the central hub or switch can be a single point of failure, necessitating redundancy measures for critical networks.

3) Ring: Ring topology offers predictable and consistent network performance, as each node is connected to exactly two other nodes, forming a closed loop. This topology minimizes data collisions, but its performance can be affected by the failure of a single node, requiring fault-tolerant mechanisms.

4) Mesh: Mesh topology is highly resilient, as multiple paths exist between nodes, ensuring data can be transmitted even if some connections fail. This redundancy increases network reliability but comes at the cost of increased complexity and cabling requirements.

5) Hybrid: Hybrid topology combines the advantages of multiple topologies to create a network tailored to specific needs. For instance, a network could use a star topology for connecting multiple departments and a mesh topology for connecting critical devices, ensuring high performance and fault tolerance.

Network topologies significantly impact the design, performance, and reliability of a network. Administrators must consider factors such as scalability, cost, complexity, and redundancy when selecting the optimal topology for a given network.

Network Protocols

Network protocols define the rules and conventions for communication within a network. Some essential network protocols include:

Internet Protocol (IP) is a fundamental network protocol that assigns unique addresses to each device connected to a network, allowing them to communicate with one another. IP is responsible for routing data packets across networks, ensuring that information is transmitted to its intended destination. The two primary versions of IP are IPv4 and IPv6, with IPv6 gradually replacing IPv4 due to its larger address space.

Transmission Control Protocol (TCP) is another essential protocol that guarantees reliable, ordered, and error-checked data transmission between devices. TCP establishes a connection between nodes, ensuring that data packets are delivered without loss or corruption. It also manages flow control and congestion on the network, contributing to overall stability and performance.

User Datagram Protocol (UDP) is a connectionless transport protocol that offers fast data transmission with minimal error-checking, making it suitable for applications where low latency is more important than data integrity, such as online gaming or live video streaming. Unlike TCP, UDP does not establish a connection, nor does it guarantee packet delivery.

Hypertext Transfer Protocol (HTTP) and its secure counterpart, HTTPS, facilitate communication between web browsers and servers. HTTP is the foundation of data communication on the World Wide Web, allowing users to access and interact with web pages. HTTPS adds a layer of security to HTTP through encryption, protecting data transmitted between the browser and server.

File Transfer Protocol (FTP) is a standard protocol used for transferring files between devices on a network. FTP allows users to upload, download, and manage files on a remote server, enabling efficient file sharing and collaboration. Secure versions of FTP, such as FTPS and SFTP, incorporate encryption to protect sensitive data during transmission.

Simple Mail Transfer Protocol (SMTP) and Internet Message Access Protocol (IMAP) are email protocols that govern the transmission and retrieval of email messages. SMTP is responsible for sending emails from a client to a server or between servers, while IMAP enables users to access and manage their emails on a remote mail server.

The OSI Model

The Open Systems Interconnection (OSI) model is a vital conceptual framework that categorizes the functions of a network into seven distinct layers. Gaining a thorough understanding of the OSI model is critical for network administrators, as it streamlines the process of troubleshooting network issues by enabling the isolation of problems to specific layers.

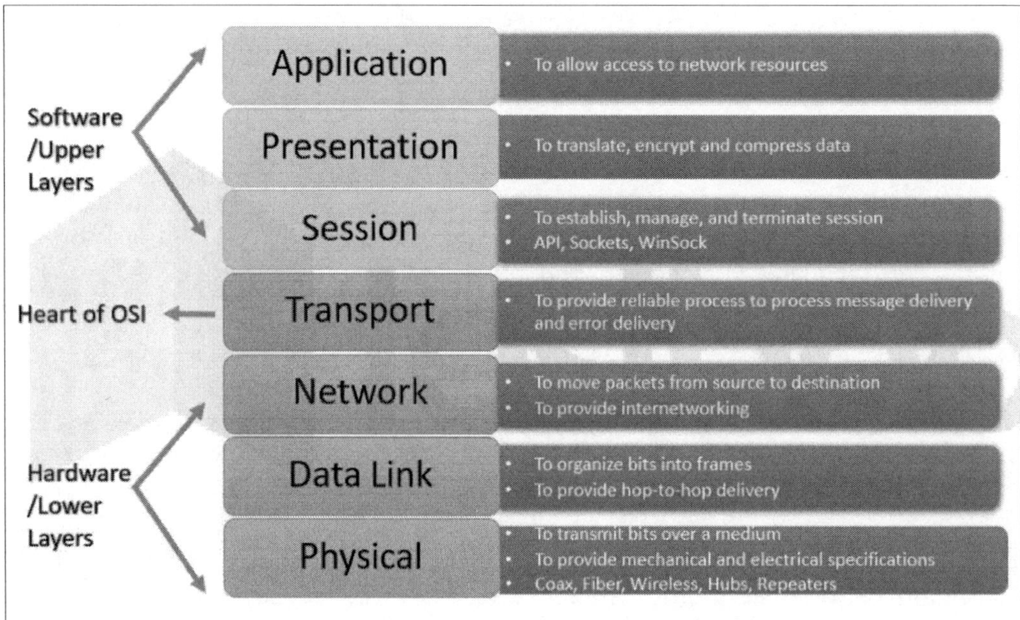

The seven layers of the OSI model are as follows:

1) Physical (Layer 1): This layer is responsible for the transmission of raw bits over a physical medium, such as cables or radio waves. It also deals with the physical connections between devices, electrical signaling, and synchronization.

2) Data Link (Layer 2): The Data Link layer establishes and maintains reliable communication between adjacent nodes on a network. It is in charge of error detection and correction, as well as organizing data into frames for transmission.

3) Network (Layer 3): This layer handles routing and forwarding of data between different networks. It is responsible for determining the best path for data packets based on factors like the shortest distance, lowest cost, or least congestion.

4) Transport (Layer 4): The Transport layer provides reliable, error-checked data transmission between nodes. It manages flow control and congestion management, ensuring that data is transmitted and received in an orderly and efficient manner.

5) Session (Layer 5): The Session layer manages the establishment, maintenance, and termination of connections between nodes. It is responsible for coordinating communication sessions, controlling data exchange, and recovering from failures.

6) Presentation (Layer 6): This layer translates data between application and network formats, handling tasks such as data compression, encryption, and character encoding. It ensures that data is presented in a format that both the sender and receiver can understand.

7) Application (Layer 7): The Application layer represents the interface between the user and the network, providing high-level services such as email, web browsing, and file transfers. It acts as a mediator between users and network processes, enabling seamless communication and resource sharing.

The OSI model serves as a valuable tool for understanding and managing complex network systems, ultimately enhancing the overall performance and reliability of the network.

IP Addressing

IP addresses serve as unique identifiers for each device within a network, allowing them to communicate and exchange data effectively. Two primary versions of IP addressing exist:

- IPv4, a 32-bit address format, consists of four decimal numbers separated by periods (e.g., 192.168.1.1). While widely used, the limited address space of IPv4 has necessitated a gradual transition to IPv6.

- The IPv6 format, with its 128-bit address space, offers a significantly larger pool of addresses. These addresses are represented as eight groups of four hexadecimal digits separated by colons (e.g., 2001:0db8:85a3:0000:0000:8a2e:0370:7334).

IP addresses can be assigned in two ways: statically or dynamically. Static IP addresses are manually assigned by network administrators, whereas dynamic IP addresses are automatically assigned by a Dynamic Host Configuration Protocol (DHCP) server. This server streamlines address management and ensures each device on the network receives a unique IP address. Furthermore, IP addresses are categorized as either public or private. Public IP addresses are globally unique and routable across the Internet, while private IP addresses are reserved for use within local networks, enhancing security and enabling devices to communicate internally without direct exposure to the public Internet.

Subnetting

Subnetting is the process of dividing an IP network into smaller sub networks or "subnets." Subnetting improves network efficiency and security by limiting the broadcast domain and isolating network traffic. A subnet mask is used to determine the network portion of an IP address, with the remaining bits representing the host portion.

Routing and Switching

Routing and switching are core functions of a network:

- Switching: Switches operate at Layer 2 (Data Link) of the OSI model, forwarding data frames based on their Media Access Control (MAC) addresses. Switches maintain a MAC address table, learning the addresses of connected devices and intelligently forwarding data to the appropriate destination.

- Routing: Routers operate at Layer 3 (Network) of the OSI model, forwarding data packets between networks based on their IP addresses. Routers maintain a routing table, determining the best path for data transmission based on factors such as the number of hops, latency, and bandwidth.

Network Security

Network security is of paramount importance in today's interconnected world, as it safeguards sensitive data and upholds the integrity of computer networks. A variety of network security measures have been developed to ensure the safety and privacy of information transmitted across networks.

Firewalls are essential components of network security, acting as a barrier between internal and external networks. They can be implemented as standalone devices or as software installed on network devices. Firewalls filter incoming and outgoing traffic based on predefined rules, preventing unauthorized access and protecting the network from various cyber threats.

Intrusion Detection Systems (IDS) and Intrusion Prevention Systems (IPS) play a significant role in maintaining network security. These systems continuously monitor network traffic, detecting and analyzing suspicious activities. IDS focuses on identifying potential threats and alerting administrators, while IPS actively blocks or mitigates malicious traffic in real-time, providing an extra layer of protection against cyberattacks.

Virtual Private Networks (VPNs) are crucial for securing data transmitted over public networks, such as the Internet. By creating encrypted tunnels between network endpoints, VPNs ensure the confidentiality and integrity of data, preventing eavesdropping, tampering, and unauthorized access.

Access control is another key aspect of network security, as it limits network access to authorized users and devices. This can be achieved through various methods, including the use of authentication protocols, role-based access control, and network segmentation. By implementing access control measures, network administrators can minimize the risk of unauthorized access and ensure that only trusted users and devices can access sensitive resources.

Network Monitoring and Troubleshooting

Network administrators must monitor network performance and troubleshoot issues as they arise. Common network monitoring and troubleshooting tools include:

1) Ping: Tests network connectivity between devices by sending ICMP echo request packets and measuring response times.

2) Traceroute: Maps the path data takes between two nodes, identifying intermediate devices and potential bottlenecks.

3) Wireshark: Captures and analyzes network packets, providing detailed insights into network traffic.

4) Network analyzers and monitoring software: Collect and display real-time network performance metrics, helping administrators identify issues and optimize network performance.

With this foundation, you can begin to explore the practical applications of networking using Python and build the skills required to become a successful network administrator. To me, knowing this foundation is itself an achievement and a starting point to the career of a networking professional.

Summary

In the first chapter of "Python Networking 101," we covered the fundamentals of networking, providing a solid foundation for aspiring network administrators. We began by exploring the key components of a computer network, including nodes, communication media, networking hardware, and networking software. We then discussed various network types, such as Personal Area Networks (PANs), Local Area Networks (LANs), Wide Area Networks (WANs), and Virtual Private Networks (VPNs), as well as network topologies like bus, star, ring, mesh, and hybrid configurations.

Next, we delved into essential network protocols, such as Internet Protocol (IP), Transmission Control Protocol (TCP), User Datagram Protocol (UDP), Hypertext Transfer Protocol (HTTP), File Transfer Protocol (FTP), and email protocols like SMTP and IMAP. We also introduced the Open Systems Interconnection (OSI) model, a seven-layer conceptual framework that standardizes network functions and assists in troubleshooting network issues. Furthermore, we discussed IP addressing, including IPv4 and IPv6, static and dynamic addressing, and public and private addresses, as well as subnetting and its role in improving network efficiency and security.

Lastly, we touched upon the core functions of routing and switching, network security measures such as firewalls, IDS/IPS, VPNs, and access control, and the importance of network monitoring and troubleshooting using tools like ping, traceroute, Wireshark, and network analyzers. With this foundational knowledge, readers are well-prepared to explore the practical applications of networking using Python and develop the skills necessary for a successful career as a network administrator.

Chapter 2: TCP, UDP and Socket Programming

In this chapter, we will delve deeper into network protocols and layers, exploring their concepts and learning how to implement them using Python's socket programming. We will discuss some essential network protocols in detail, understand the layers at which they operate, and practice writing simple Python scripts to work with these protocols.

This chapter and various topics covered in it will provide a comprehensive understanding of network protocols and layers, along with hands-on experience in implementing them using Python's socket programming. This knowledge will enable you to develop more complex networking applications and further hone your skills as a network administrator. Let us explore and learn!

Transport Layer Protocols: TCP and UDP

The transport layer, also known as Layer 4 in the OSI model, is responsible for providing end-to-end communication services between applications running on different devices within a network. It ensures reliable and efficient data transfer by implementing various error detection, flow control, and congestion control mechanisms. The two primary transport layer protocols are the Transmission Control Protocol (TCP) and the User Datagram Protocol (UDP). In this section, we will discuss both protocols in detail, highlighting their key features, similarities, and differences.

Transmission Control Protocol (TCP)

TCP is a connection-oriented, reliable, and full-duplex transport layer protocol. It ensures that data is delivered accurately and in the correct order, making it suitable for applications that require high reliability, such as web browsing, file transfers, and email.

Key Features of TCP

- Connection-Oriented: TCP establishes a connection between the sender and receiver before transmitting data. This connection is maintained throughout the communication process until both parties have finished exchanging data.

- Reliable: TCP uses error detection mechanisms, such as checksums and sequence numbers, to ensure that data is transmitted accurately and in the correct order. If a packet is lost or corrupted during transmission, the recipient can request retransmission.

- Flow Control: TCP manages the rate of data transmission between sender and receiver to prevent overloading the recipient's buffer. This is achieved using a sliding window mechanism, which allows the sender to transmit data only when the receiver has available buffer space.

- Congestion Control: TCP monitors network congestion and adjusts the transmission rate accordingly, preventing packet loss and ensuring efficient use of network resources. This is achieved through mechanisms like slow start, congestion avoidance, fast retransmit, and fast recovery.

- Full-Duplex: TCP supports simultaneous data transmission in both directions, allowing the sender and receiver to exchange data concurrently.

User Datagram Protocol (UDP)

UDP is a connectionless, unreliable, and lightweight transport layer protocol. It does not guarantee the delivery, order, or integrity of data, making it suitable for applications that prioritize speed and simplicity over reliability, such as streaming media, online gaming, and Voice over IP (VoIP).

Key Features of UDP:

- Connectionless: Unlike TCP, UDP does not establish a connection before transmitting data. Instead, it sends datagrams independently, without maintaining a connection between sender and receiver.

- Unreliable: UDP does not provide error detection, flow control, or congestion control mechanisms. As a result, it cannot guarantee the delivery, order, or integrity of data. However, this simplicity allows for faster data transmission and lower overhead.

- Lightweight: UDP has a smaller header size compared to TCP, resulting in less overhead and faster processing. This makes it an ideal choice for applications that require minimal latency.

- No Flow Control or Congestion Control: As UDP does not implement flow control or congestion control mechanisms, it can send data as quickly as the sender generates it. This is beneficial for real-time applications, such as video streaming or online gaming, where occasional packet loss is acceptable.

Comparing TCP and UDP

Reliability: TCP is a reliable protocol that guarantees data delivery, order, and integrity. In contrast, UDP is an unreliable protocol that does not provide any such guarantees.

Connection: TCP is connection-oriented, establishing a connection before data transmission. UDP is connectionless, sending data without prior connection establishment.

Flow Control and Congestion Control: TCP implements flow control and congestion control mechanisms, ensuring efficient use of network resources and preventing buffer overflows. UDP does not provide any such features.

Speed and Overhead: TCP has higher overhead due to its error detection, flow control, and congestion control mechanisms, resulting in slower data transmission. UDP has lower overhead and faster transmission, making it suitable for applications that prioritize speed and minimal latency.

Use Cases: TCP is ideal for applications that require high reliability, such as web browsing, file transfers, and email. UDP is suitable for applications that can tolerate occasional packet loss and prioritize speed, such as streaming media, online gaming, and VoIP.

In summary, both TCP and UDP serve different purposes and are suitable for different types of applications. TCP is the go-to protocol when reliability, data integrity, and order are crucial, while UDP is preferred for applications that prioritize speed and low latency. It is essential for network administrators to understand the differences between these two transport layer protocols to make informed decisions when configuring and troubleshooting networks.

Socket Programming in Python

Sockets are the fundamental building blocks of network communication and play a crucial role in establishing connections between devices. They provide an interface for applications to send and receive data over networks. Understanding the basics and types of sockets is essential before diving into socket programming in Python.

Basics of Sockets

A socket is an endpoint in a network communication process that enables data exchange between two devices. It is associated with a unique combination of an IP address and a port number, which together identify a specific process running on a device. Sockets enable applications to send and receive data using transport layer protocols like TCP and UDP.

There are two primary operations performed by sockets: listening and connecting. A server socket listens for incoming connections from client sockets, while client sockets initiate connections to server sockets. Once a connection is established, data can be transmitted bidirectionally between the server and client.

Sockets can be broadly classified into two categories based on the transport layer protocol they use: stream sockets and datagram sockets.

Stream Sockets (TCP Sockets)

Stream sockets use the Transmission Control Protocol (TCP) for communication. They are connection-oriented, meaning that a connection is established between the sender and receiver before data transmission. Stream sockets ensure reliable, in-order, and error-free communication, making them suitable for applications that require high reliability, such as web browsing, file transfers, and email.

Some key characteristics of stream sockets are:
- Reliable: They guarantee accurate, in-order, and error-free data transmission.
- Connection-oriented: A connection must be established before data can be exchanged.
- Full-duplex: They allow simultaneous data transmission in both directions.
- Suitable for applications requiring high reliability and accurate data transmission.

Datagram Sockets (UDP Sockets)

Datagram sockets use the User Datagram Protocol (UDP) for communication. They are connectionless, meaning that data is transmitted independently without establishing a connection between sender and receiver. Datagram sockets are suitable for applications that prioritize speed and simplicity over reliability, such as streaming media, online gaming, and Voice over IP (VoIP).

Some key characteristics of datagram sockets are:
- Unreliable: They do not guarantee data delivery, order, or integrity.
- Connectionless: No connection is established before data transmission.
- Lightweight: They have a smaller header size compared to stream sockets, resulting in lower overhead and faster processing.
- Suitable for applications requiring minimal latency and fast data transmission.

Understanding the basics and types of sockets is essential for successful socket programming in Python. Stream sockets (TCP) and datagram sockets (UDP) cater to different types of applications based on their reliability, connection orientation, and latency requirements. By choosing the appropriate socket type, you can develop efficient network applications that meet the specific needs of various use cases.

Python Socket Library

Python provides a built-in library called 'socket' that makes it easy to perform network programming tasks, such as creating, connecting, and managing sockets. The socket library provides various functions and classes for working with both TCP (stream) and UDP (datagram) sockets. In this section, we will learn about the socket library and how to use it for socket programming in Python.

Importing Socket Library

To start using the socket library, you need to import it at the beginning of your Python script:

```
import socket
```

Creating a Socket in Python

To create a socket in Python, you can use the socket.socket() function provided by the socket library. This function takes two arguments: the address family (AF) and the socket type (SOCK). The address family is used to specify the protocol family (IPv4 or IPv6), and the socket type is used to specify the transport layer protocol (TCP or UDP).

For example, to create a TCP socket using IPv4, you would call the socket.socket() function like this:

```
tcp_socket = socket.socket(socket.AF_INET, socket.SOCK_STREAM)
```

Similarly, to create a UDP socket using IPv4, you would use the following code:

```
udp_socket = socket.socket(socket.AF_INET, socket.SOCK_DGRAM)
```

Binding Socket to IP Address and Port

Before a server socket can listen for incoming connections, it must be bound to an IP address and port number. This can be done using the bind() method of the socket object. The bind() method takes a single argument, a tuple containing the IP address and port number.

For example, to bind a socket to the IP address '127.0.0.1' and port number 12345, you would use the following code:

```
address = ('127.0.0.1', 12345)
tcp_socket.bind(address)
```

Closing a Socket

When you are done using a socket, it is important to close it using the close() method. This frees up system resources and prevents potential conflicts with other applications.

```
tcp_socket.close()
```

Now that you have a basic understanding of the socket library and how to create, bind, and close sockets in Python, you are ready to explore more advanced topics, such as establishing connections, sending and receiving data, and implementing server and client applications using TCP and UDP sockets.

TCP Socket Programming

Now, let us learn and practice to establish TCP connections, send and receive data over TCP, and terminate a TCP connection using Python's socket library.

Establishing a TCP Connection

To establish a TCP connection, the server must first create a socket, bind it to an IP address and port, and then start listening for incoming client connections. The following steps demonstrate how to achieve this:

Create a socket:

```
import socket
server_socket = socket.socket(socket.AF_INET, socket.SOCK_STREAM)
```

Bind the socket to an IP address and port:

```
address = ('127.0.0.1', 12345)
server_socket.bind(address)
```

Listen for incoming connections:

```python
server_socket.listen(5) # The argument (5) is the maximum number of queued connections.
```

Accept an incoming connection:

```python
client_socket, client_address = server_socket.accept()
print(f"Connection established with {client_address}")
```

On the client-side, you need to create a socket and connect to the server's IP address and port.

Create a socket:

```python
import socket
client_socket = socket.socket(socket.AF_INET, socket.SOCK_STREAM)
```

Connect to the server:

```python
server_address = ('127.0.0.1', 12345)
client_socket.connect(server_address)
```

Sending and Receiving Data over TCP

Once a connection is established, you can use the send() and recv() methods to transmit and receive data over TCP.

Sending Data:

To send data, you can use the send() method of the socket object. This method takes a single argument, the data to be sent, which must be a bytes-like object.

Example (Client-Side):

```python
data = "Hello, Server!"
```

```
client_socket.send(data.encode()) # Convert the string to bytes and send it.
```

Receiving Data:

To receive data, you can use the recv() method of the socket object. This method takes a single argument, the maximum amount of data (in bytes) to receive, and returns the received data as a bytes-like object.

Example (Server-Side):

```
data = server_socket.recv(1024) # Receive up to 1024 bytes of data.
print(f"Received data: {data.decode()}") # Convert the bytes to a string and print it.
```

Terminating a TCP Connection

To close a TCP connection, both the server and client should close their respective sockets using the close() method.

Server-Side:

```
client_socket.close()
server_socket.close()
```

Client-Side:

```
client_socket.close()
```

In the simplest terms, to execute TCP socket programming in Python, you will first need to build and bind a socket, then establish a connection, then send and receive data, and lastly close the connection.

Implementing a TCP Server and Client

Considering so far what we learned, we can start with creating a simple TCP server and client using Python's socket library. The server will listen for incoming client connections, receive a message from the client, print the received message, and send a response back to the client.

TCP Server

Create a file named "tcp_server.py" and add the following code:

```python
import socket

# Create a socket
server_socket = socket.socket(socket.AF_INET, socket.SOCK_STREAM)

# Bind the socket to an IP address and port
address = ('127.0.0.1', 12345)
server_socket.bind(address)

# Listen for incoming connections
server_socket.listen(5)
print("Server listening on", address)

while True:
    # Accept an incoming connection
    client_socket, client_address = server_socket.accept()
    print(f"Connection established with {client_address}")

    # Receive data from the client
    data = client_socket.recv(1024)
    print(f"Received data: {data.decode()}")

    # Send a response back to the client
    response = "Hello, Client!"
    client_socket.send(response.encode())

    # Close the client socket
    client_socket.close()

# Close the server socket (unreachable in this particular   sample program)
```

```python
server_socket.close()
```

TCP Client

Create a file named "tcp_client.py" and add the following code:

```python
import socket

# Create a socket
client_socket = socket.socket(socket.AF_INET, socket.SOCK_STREAM)

# Connect to the server
server_address = ('127.0.0.1', 12345)
client_socket.connect(server_address)
print(f"Connected to server at {server_address}")

# Send data to the server
data = "Hello, Server!"
client_socket.send(data.encode())

# Receive data from the server
response = client_socket.recv(1024)
print(f"Received data: {response.decode()}")

# Close the client socket
client_socket.close()
```

Running the TCP Server and Client

To run the TCP server and client, follow these steps:

Open two terminal windows.

In the first terminal, navigate to the directory containing "tcp_server.py" and run the following command:

```
python tcp_server.py
```

The server will start listening for incoming connections.

In the second terminal, navigate to the directory containing "tcp_client.py" and run the following command:

```
python tcp_client.py
```

The client will connect to the server, send a message, receive a response, and print the received data.

Observe the output in both terminals. The server should display the connection details and the received message, while the client should display the connection details and the received response.

Creating a TCP server and client in Python requires establishing connections, binding sockets, transmitting and receiving data, and finally closing the connections. Additionally, you will need to create sockets and bind them. If you follow these instructions, you will be able to construct a wide variety of server and client applications that take advantage of the connection-oriented and reliable characteristics offered by the TCP protocol.

UDP Socket Programming in Python

Similar to TCP socket programming, we will also learn about UDP socket programming in Python, including establishing a UDP connection, working with connectionless sockets, and sending and receiving data over UDP. We will use a similar example as used in the previous section, with a server that listens for incoming messages and sends a response back to the client.

Establishing a UDP Connection

Unlike TCP, UDP is a connectionless protocol, meaning there is no need to establish a connection between the server and client. Instead, the server and client simply send and receive data without establishing a formal connection.

Working with Connectionless Sockets

To create a UDP server, you need to create a socket, bind it to an IP address and port, and start listening for incoming datagrams. The following steps demonstrate how to achieve this:

Create a socket:

```
import socket
server_socket = socket.socket(socket.AF_INET, socket.SOCK_DGRAM)
```

Bind the socket to an IP address and port:

```
address = ('127.0.0.1', 12345)
server_socket.bind(address)
```

On the client-side, you need to create a socket, and you can directly send and receive data without connecting to the server.

Create a socket:

```
import socket
client_socket = socket.socket(socket.AF_INET, socket.SOCK_DGRAM)
```

Sending and Receiving Data over UDP

Sending Data:

To send data over UDP, you can use the sendto() method of the socket object. This method takes two arguments: the data to be sent (a bytes-like object) and the destination address (a tuple containing the IP address and port number).

Example (Client-Side):

```
data = "Hello, Server!"
server_address = ('127.0.0.1', 12345)
client_socket.sendto(data.encode(), server_address)
```

Receiving Data:

To receive data over UDP, you can use the recvfrom() method of the socket object. This method takes a single argument, the maximum amount of data (in bytes) to receive, and returns the received data as a bytes-like object and the source address.

Example (Server-Side):

```
data, client_address = server_socket.recvfrom(1024)
print(f"Received data: {data.decode()} from {client_address}")
```

Implementing a UDP Server and Client

UDP Server

Create a file named "udp_server.py" and add the following code:

```
import socket

# Create a socket
server_socket = socket.socket(socket.AF_INET, socket.SOCK_DGRAM)

# Bind the socket to an IP address and port
address = ('127.0.0.1', 12345)
server_socket.bind(address)
print("Server listening on", address)

while True:
    # Receive data from the client
    data, client_address = server_socket.recvfrom(1024)
    print(f"Received data: {data.decode()} from {client_address}")

    # Send a response back to the client
    response = "Hello, Client!"
    server_socket.sendto(response.encode(), client_address)
```

UDP Client

Create a file named "udp_client.py" and add the following code:

```python
import socket

# Create a socket
client_socket = socket.socket(socket.AF_INET, socket.SOCK_DGRAM)

# Send data to the server
data = "Hello, Server!"
server_address = ('127.0.0.1', 12345)
client_socket.sendto(data.encode(), server_address)

# Receive data from the server
response, server_address = client_socket.recvfrom(1024)
print(f"Received data: {response.decode()} from {server_address}")

Close the client socket
client_socket.close()
```

Running the UDP Server and Client

To run the UDP server and client, follow these steps:

Open two terminal windows.

In the first terminal, navigate to the directory containing "udp_server.py" and run the following command:

```
python udp_server.py
```

The server will start listening for incoming datagrams.

In the second terminal, navigate to the directory containing "udp_client.py" and run the following command:

```
python udp_client.py
```

The client will send a message to the server and receive a response, printing the received data.

Observe the output in both terminals. The server should display the received message and the client's address, while the client should display the received response and the server's address.

Writing a UDP socket in Python is far less complicated than writing a TCP socket in Python due to the fact that there is no need to create a connection between the server and the client. You can construct server and client programs that take use of the speed and simplicity offered by the UDP protocol by employing connectionless sockets to communicate with one another via the methods 'sendto()' and 'recvfrom()'.

Summary

Understanding network protocols and layers, as well as socket programming in Python, were the primary focuses of this chapter. We started off by conducting some conceptual research on network protocols and the significance of these protocols in terms of their role in facilitating communication between devices on a network. Following that, we dove deeper into the specifics of transport layer protocols, specifically TCP and UDP, due to the significant impact that they have on networking.

Transmission Control Protocol, also known simply as TCP, is a connection-oriented protocol that ensures the delivery of data in an ordered and reliable fashion. We learned about the process of closing a connection, the three-way handshake that is required to establish a connection, the flow control and congestion control mechanisms that ensure data integrity, and the process of establishing a connection in the first place.
User Datagram Protocol, also known as UDP, is a connectionless and lightweight protocol that offers more rapid data transmission at the expense of reliability. We went over the key differences between TCP and UDP, as well as how each protocol is best suited for specific kinds of applications.

Following that, we moved on to the Python socket programming, which gives us the ability to create network applications by utilizing the built-in socket library. We began by gaining an understanding of the fundamentals of sockets, which included the different types of sockets (TCP and UDP), as well as the procedure for creating, binding, and listening for connections. Through the study of TCP socket programming, we became familiar with the processes of establishing connections, sending and receiving data over TCP, and closing a TCP connection. For the purpose of demonstrating these concepts, we built a straightforward TCP server and client. Following that, we went on to study how to program using UDP sockets, which entails working with connectionless sockets and transmitting and receiving data using UDP. We went over the fundamental steps involved in creating and binding sockets, as well as sending data with the sendto() method and receiving data with the recvfrom() method. In order to better illustrate the concepts, we also implemented a straightforward UDP server and client. In a nutshell, this chapter laid a solid groundwork for future study in Python's socket programming and provided an overview of network protocols and layers.

Chapter 3: Working with Application Layer

In this chapter, we will explore various Application Layer Protocols, which are crucial for the functioning of the internet and network applications. We will discuss HTTP, HTTPS, FTP, SMTP, IMAP, and DNS in detail.

Overview of Application Layer Protocols

HTTP (Hypertext Transfer Protocol)

HTTP is the foundation of data communication on the World Wide Web. It is a request-response protocol that enables clients (usually web browsers) to request resources (such as web pages, images, and videos) from servers. HTTP uses a stateless connection, meaning each request and response pair is independent and doesn't rely on previous connections. The protocol operates primarily over TCP, using port 80 by default.

HTTPS (Hypertext Transfer Protocol Secure)

HTTPS is a secure version of HTTP that uses encryption to ensure the confidentiality and integrity of data transmitted between the client and server. It employs Transport Layer Security (TLS) or its predecessor, Secure Sockets Layer (SSL), to encrypt the data. HTTPS operates over TCP, using port 443 by default, and is widely used for sensitive data transmission, such as online banking, e-commerce, and login pages.

FTP (File Transfer Protocol)

FTP is a standard network protocol used to transfer files between a client and a server over a TCP-based network, such as the Internet. FTP uses a client-server architecture and employs separate control and data connections to facilitate the transfer of files, making it more efficient and reliable. The protocol operates over TCP, using ports 20 and 21 for data and control connections, respectively.

SMTP (Simple Mail Transfer Protocol)

SMTP is an Internet standard for email transmission across IP networks. It is a text-based protocol that allows mail servers to send, receive, and relay email messages. SMTP operates over TCP, using port 25 by default, and provides the basic framework for email communication, although it is often used in conjunction with other protocols like IMAP and POP3 for receiving and managing email.

IMAP (Internet Message Access Protocol)

IMAP is an Internet standard protocol used to access and manage email on a remote mail server. Unlike POP3, which downloads and deletes email from the server, IMAP allows users to access and manipulate their email directly on the server, making it more suitable for managing email across multiple devices. IMAP operates over TCP, using port 143 by default, or port 993 for secure IMAP (IMAPS) connections.

DNS (Domain Name System)

DNS is a hierarchical and decentralized naming system for computers, services, or other resources connected to the Internet or a private network. It translates human-readable domain names (like www.example.com) into the IP addresses (like 192.0.2.1) required for identifying and locating devices and services on a network. DNS operates primarily over UDP, using port 53, but can also use TCP for larger queries or zone transfers.

In this chapter, we will dive deeper into each of these Application Layer Protocols, understanding their purpose, architecture, and how they interact with other protocols to provide essential functionality for network applications.

HTTP/HTTPS Requests and Responses

HTTP (Hypertext Transfer Protocol) is the backbone of data communication on the World Wide Web. It is a request-response protocol that allows clients (usually web browsers) to request resources (such as web pages, images, and videos) from servers. HTTP operates primarily over TCP, using port 80 by default.

HTTPS (Hypertext Transfer Protocol Secure) is a secure version of HTTP that employs encryption to ensure the confidentiality and integrity of data transmitted between the client and server. It uses Transport Layer Security (TLS) or its predecessor, Secure Sockets Layer (SSL), to encrypt the data. HTTPS operates over TCP, using port 443 by default, and is widely used for sensitive data transmission, such as online banking, e-commerce, and login pages.

Python's Requests Library

Python's Requests library is a popular library for making HTTP requests. It simplifies the process of sending requests and handling responses, making it easy to interact with web services and retrieve data from the internet. The library offers various useful features such as handling redirects, following links in web pages, and submitting forms.

To install the Requests library, use the following pip command:

```
pip install requests
```

Sending a GET Request

A GET request is used to retrieve data from a server. To send a GET request using the Requests library, use the get() function:

```python
import requests

response = requests.get('https://www.example.com')
print(response.text)
```

The get() function returns a Response object, which contains the server's response to the request. The text attribute of the Response object contains the response content as a string.

Sending a POST Request

A POST request is used to send data to a server. To send a POST request using the Requests library, use the post() function:

```python
import requests

data = {'username': 'example', 'password': 'example_password'}
response = requests.post('https://www.example.com/login', data=data)
print(response.text)
```

The post() function takes an optional data parameter, which is a dictionary containing the data to be sent to the server.

Handling Response Status Codes

The Response object also contains the HTTP status code returned by the server. You can use the raise_for_status() method to check if the request was successful:

```python
import requests

response = requests.get('https://www.example.com')
response.raise_for_status()  # Raises an exception if the request was unsuccessful
print(response.text)
```

<u>Working with JSON Data</u>

The Requests library makes it easy to work with JSON data. To parse JSON data from a response, use the json() method of the Response object:

```python
import requests

response = requests.get('https://api.example.com/data')
data = response.json()
print(data)
```

<u>Adding Headers to Requests</u>

You can add custom headers to requests by passing a dictionary of headers to the headers parameter:

```python
import requests

headers = {'User-Agent': 'my-app'}
response = requests.get('https://www.example.com', headers=headers)
print(response.text)
```

As we witnessed, Python's Requests library simplifies the process of making HTTP requests and handling responses. By using its various functions and methods, you can easily interact with web services and retrieve data from the internet, making it a valuable tool in the networking domain.

Performing FTP Operations

FTP (File Transfer Protocol) is a standard network protocol used to transfer files between a client and a server over a TCP-based network, such as the Internet. FTP uses a client-server architecture and employs separate control and data connections to facilitate the transfer of files, making it more efficient and reliable. The protocol operates over TCP, using ports 20 and 21 for data and control connections, respectively.

<u>Python's ftplib</u>

Python's ftplib is a built-in library that provides tools for working with FTP servers. It offers an easy-to-use interface for connecting to FTP servers, navigating directories, and uploading and downloading files.

Connecting to FTP Server

To connect to an FTP server, create an instance of the FTP class and use the connect() and login() methods:

```python
from ftplib import FTP


ftp = FTP()
ftp.connect('ftp.example.com', 21)  # Connect to the FTP server
ftp.login('username', 'password')  # Log in with your credentials
print(ftp.getwelcome())  # Print the server's welcome message
```

Listing Directories and Files

To list the contents of a directory, use the dir() method:

```python
from ftplib import FTP


# ... (connect and log in to the FTP server)


ftp.dir()  # List the contents of the current directory
```

Changing Directories

To change the current working directory on the server, use the cwd() method:

```python
from ftplib import FTP


# ... (connect and log in to the FTP server)


ftp.cwd('/path/to/directory')  # Change the current working directory
```

Creating and Removing Directories

To create a new directory, use the mkd() method. To remove a directory, use the rmd() method:

```python
from ftplib import FTP

# ... (connect and log in to the FTP server)

ftp.mkd('/path/to/new/directory')  # Create a new directory
ftp.rmd('/path/to/directory')  # Remove a directory
```

Uploading Files

To upload a file to the server, use the storbinary() method:

```python
from ftplib import FTP

# ... (connect and log in to the FTP server)

with open('local_file.txt', 'rb') as f:
    ftp.storbinary('STOR remote_file.txt', f)  # Upload the file to the server
```

Downloading Files

To download a file from the server, use the retrbinary() method:

```python
from ftplib import FTP

# ... (connect and log in to the FTP server)

with open('local_file.txt', 'wb') as f:
    ftp.retrbinary('RETR remote_file.txt', f.write)  # Download the file from the
server
```

Disconnecting from Server

To close the connection to the server, use the quit() method:

```python
from ftplib import FTP

# ... (connect and log in to the FTP server and perform operations)

ftp.quit()  # Disconnect from the server
```

The ftplib module in Python provides a user-friendly interface for communicating with FTP hosts. Those who work with FTP, will find it useful because it makes connecting to servers, navigating directories, downloading and uploading files, and managing download queues much simpler.

Sending and Receiving Emails

SMTP (Simple Mail Transfer Protocol) is an Internet standard for email transmission across IP networks. It is a text-based protocol that allows mail servers to send, receive, and relay email messages. SMTP operates over TCP, using port 25 by default, and provides the basic framework for email communication, although it is often used in conjunction with other protocols like IMAP and POP3 for receiving and managing email.

IMAP (Internet Message Access Protocol) is an Internet standard protocol used to access and manage email on a remote mail server. Unlike POP3, which downloads and deletes email from the server, IMAP allows users to access and manipulate their email directly on the server, making it more suitable for managing email across multiple devices. IMAP operates over TCP, using port 143 by default, or port 993 for secure IMAP (IMAPS) connections.

Exploring smtplib and imaplib

Smtplib is a built-in Python library that provides tools for working with SMTP servers. It offers an easy-to-use interface for sending email messages through SMTP servers.

Imaplib is a built-in Python library that provides tools for working with IMAP servers. It offers an interface for connecting to IMAP servers, navigating mailboxes, and managing email messages.

Sending Email using smtplib

To send an email using smtplib, follow these steps:

Import the necessary libraries:

```python
import smtplib
from email.message import EmailMessage
```

Create an EmailMessage object and set its properties:

```python
msg = EmailMessage()
msg.set_content('This is the body of the email')

msg['Subject'] = 'Test Email'
msg['From'] = 'sender@example.com'
msg['To'] = 'recipient@example.com'
```

Connect to the SMTP server and send the email:

```python
smtp_server = 'smtp.example.com'
smtp_port = 587  # Use the appropriate port for your SMTP server

with smtplib.SMTP(smtp_server, smtp_port) as server:
    server.starttls()  # Use TLS encryption
    server.login('username', 'password')  # Log in to the SMTP server
    server.send_message(msg)  # Send the email
```

Receiving Email using imaplib

To receive email using imaplib, follow these steps:

Import the necessary libraries:

```python
import imaplib
```

```python
import email
```

Connect to the IMAP server and log in:

```python
imap_server = 'imap.example.com'
imap_port = 993  # Use the appropriate port for your IMAP server

mail = imaplib.IMAP4_SSL(imap_server, imap_port)
mail.login('username', 'password')
```

Select the mailbox and search for emails:

```python
mail.select('inbox')  # Select the mailbox
_, data = mail.search(None, 'ALL')  # Search for all emails in the mailbox
email_ids = data[0].split()  # Extract the email IDs from the search result
```

Fetch and parse the email messages:

```python
for email_id in email_ids:
    _, data = mail.fetch(email_id, '(RFC822)')  # Fetch the email message
    raw_email = data[0][1]  # Extract the raw email data
    msg = email.message_from_bytes(raw_email)  # Parse the email message

    print('Subject:', msg['subject'])
    print('From:', msg['from'])
    print('To:', msg['to'])
    print('Body:', msg.get_payload(decode=True).decode('utf-8'))
```

Log out and close the connection:

```python
mail.logout()
```

Performing DNS Queries

DNS (Domain Name System) is a hierarchical, distributed naming system used to translate human-readable domain names (like www.example.com) into IP addresses (like 192.0.2.1) that computers can understand. It acts as a phonebook for the internet, allowing users to access websites and services using easily memorable domain names instead of having to remember numerical IP addresses. DNS operates over both UDP and TCP, using port 53 by default.

Using Socket

Python's socket library provides a simple way to perform DNS queries, which can be useful for various networking tasks, such as verifying domain names or finding the IP addresses of servers.

Import the socket library:

```
import socket
```

Use the getaddrinfo() function to perform a DNS query:
The getaddrinfo() function takes a domain name as input and returns a list of tuples containing information about the address family, socket type, protocol, and other details.

```
domain_name = 'www.example.com'
addr_info = socket.getaddrinfo(domain_name, None)

# addr_info will contain a list of tuples with address information
print(addr_info)
```

Extract IP addresses from the results:
You can loop through the addr_info list to extract the IP addresses associated with the domain name.

```
ip_addresses = []

for res in addr_info:
    ip_address = res[4][0]
```

```
    ip_addresses.append(ip_address)
# ip_addresses will contain a list of IP addresses associated with the domain name
print(ip_addresses)
```

The above example program guides and directs you to perform DNS queries using the socket library in Python. By using getaddrinfo() to query the Domain Name System, you can easily find the IP addresses associated with a given domain name.

Socket Error Handling and Troubleshooting

Socket Errors

Common socket errors can occur due to a range of factors, including network connectivity problems, misconfigurations, and server-side issues. These errors may impact the stability and functionality of network applications. Some prevalent socket errors are socket.error, socket.timeout, socket.gaierror, socket.herror, and socket.timeout. Understanding these errors and their causes is essential for developing robust network programs and implementing effective error handling techniques to ensure seamless operation, user experience, and system resilience.

Following are the common socket errors:

1) socket.error: A base class for all socket-related errors. This error occurs when a general socket error happens, which may not be covered by the more specific error classes. You should always catch this error after handling other specific socket errors.

2) socket.timeout: This error is raised when a socket operation times out. Timeouts can occur if a remote host takes too long to respond, or there is an issue with network connectivity. To handle this error, you can set a timeout value for the socket operations and catch the socket.timeout exception.

3) socket.gaierror: This error is raised when there's an address-related error, such as a failed DNS resolution. The error could be caused by an incorrect domain name, a non-existent domain, or a problem with the DNS server. To handle this error, catch the socket.gaierror exception and check the error code to determine the specific problem.

4) socket.herror: This error is raised when a host-related error occurs, such as an unknown host. This error can happen when you try to use an invalid hostname or

the host is unreachable. To handle this error, catch the socket.herror exception and check the error code to determine the specific issue.

5) socket.timeout: Raised when a socket operation times out. To handle this error, set a timeout value for the socket operations using the settimeout() method, and catch the socket.timeout exception.

Handling Socket Errors

To handle socket errors in Python, use try-except blocks. Catch the specific exceptions you want to handle and take appropriate actions, such as logging the error, retrying the operation, or gracefully shutting down the program.

Below is an example demonstrating how to handle some common socket errors:

```python
import socket

domain_name = 'www.example.com'

try:
    # Set a timeout for the socket operations
    socket.setdefaulttimeout(5)

    addr_info = socket.getaddrinfo(domain_name, None)
except socket.gaierror as e:
    if e.errno == socket.EAI_NONAME:
        print(f"Domain not found: {domain_name}")
    else:
        print(f"DNS resolution error for domain: {domain_name} - {e}")
except socket.herror as e:
    if e.errno == socket.EHOSTUNREACH:
        print(f"Host unreachable: {domain_name}")
    else:
        print(f"Host-related error for domain: {domain_name} - {e}")
except socket.timeout:
    print(f"Timeout occurred while resolving domain: {domain_name}")
```

```python
except socket.error as e:
    print(f"General socket error: {e}")
else:
    ip_addresses = [res[4][0] for res in addr_info]
    print(f"IP addresses for {domain_name}: {ip_addresses}")
```

In the above sample program, we use a try-except block to handle various socket errors while performing a DNS query. If a specific error occurs, such as a socket.gaierror or socket.herror, we print an appropriate error message. If any other general socket.error occurs, we print the error details.

Remember that it's essential to handle exceptions in the right order since Python will execute the first matching except block. As socket.error is a base class for all socket-related errors, it should be placed after the more specific exception handlers (like socket.gaierror, socket.herror, and socket.timeout) to avoid catching more specific exceptions inadvertently. Using try-except blocks to handle socket errors allows you to build more robust and resilient network programs that can handle unexpected issues gracefully and provide better user experiences.

Summary

In this chapter, we explored various Application Layer Protocols and their practical usage with Python while also discussing socket error handling. We began with HTTP and HTTPS, the foundational protocols for the World Wide Web, and learned how to use Python's requests library to perform various operations, including making HTTP requests and managing response data.

Next, we delved into the File Transfer Protocol (FTP) and demonstrated how to use Python's ftplib to perform various FTP operations, such as connecting to an FTP server and managing files. We then examined Simple Mail Transfer Protocol (SMTP) and Internet Message Access Protocol (IMAP), learning how to send and receive emails using the smtplib and imaplib libraries.

After exploring the Domain Name System (DNS) and performing DNS queries using Python's socket library, we shifted our focus to common socket errors and their handling. We discussed different socket errors, including socket.error, socket.timeout, socket.gaierror, and socket.herror, and learned how to handle them using try-except blocks in Python. We emphasized the importance of handling exceptions in the right order and understanding the specific causes of each error for building robust and resilient network programs.

CHAPTER 4: EXPLORING NETWORK AUTOMATION

Overview

Network automation refers to the process of automating the management, configuration, testing, deployment, and monitoring of network devices and their functions using software and scripting tools. In this chapter, we will explore network automation using Python and its libraries, focusing on the essential concepts and techniques.

To begin with network automation, it's crucial to understand the key concepts and components that are involved:

Network Devices: These include routers, switches, firewalls, and other devices that make up the network infrastructure. Network automation aims to manage and configure these devices efficiently and consistently.

Network Services: Network services are the functions provided by network devices, such as routing, switching, and security features. Automating these services ensures the network performs optimally and maintains its desired state.

Configuration Management: This involves maintaining a standard configuration for network devices and applying configuration changes as needed. Network automation helps keep track of these changes, ensuring that devices have the correct settings and reducing the risk of configuration-related issues.

Monitoring and Reporting: Network automation can be used to collect and analyze data from network devices, allowing administrators to monitor the health of the network and generate reports. This information can be used to identify potential issues and optimize network performance.

Python also offers a wide range of libraries that can help you automate various aspects of network management.

Some popular Python libraries for network automation include:

- Paramiko: A library for SSH and SFTP, enabling remote command execution and secure file transfers.
- Netmiko: A library that simplifies SSH-based connections to network devices and automates configuration and monitoring tasks.
- NAPALM (Network Automation and Programmability Abstraction Layer with Multivendor support): A library that provides a unified API to interact with different network devices, making it easier to manage and configure them.
- Exscript: A high-level library for automating network devices, which simplifies

connecting, configuring, and gathering information from them.
- Ansible: Although not a Python library, Ansible is a widely-used automation tool that uses Python and YAML for defining automation tasks.

As we progress through this chapter, we will dive deeper into these libraries and learn how to use them effectively for network automation tasks.

Network Automation Concepts

Network automation stands as a critical tool in the modern network administrator's kit, playing an instrumental role in efficiently managing, configuring, and maintaining network devices and services. In this section, we delve into these concepts in depth, discussing how automation can simplify complex tasks, enhance consistency, and minimize human error in configuration management. We also underscore the potential of automation in network operations, highlighting its ability to streamline workflows, improve network reliability, and free up administrators' time for strategic initiatives.

Network Devices

Network devices, such as routers, switches, and firewalls, make up the backbone of any network infrastructure. These devices have multiple functions, like routing traffic, managing VLANs, and enforcing security policies. Managing these devices manually can be time-consuming, error-prone, and inefficient.

Network automation can help address these issues by:

- Automating device discovery: By utilizing Python scripts and libraries like Nmap, you can discover devices on a network automatically, gathering their IP addresses, device types, and other relevant information.

- Configuration deployment: Network automation tools, such as Netmiko and NAPALM, allow you to deploy standardized configurations to multiple devices simultaneously, ensuring uniformity across the network.

- Backup and restoration: Automating the backup process for device configurations ensures that you always have a recent copy available for restoration in case of device failure or misconfiguration.

- Firmware upgrades: Keeping device firmware up-to-date is crucial for security and performance. Automation can help schedule and deploy firmware updates across multiple devices, reducing manual intervention and minimizing downtime.

Network Services

Network services refer to the various functions provided by network devices. These services include routing, switching, security, and Quality of Service (QoS) management. Automating these services can improve network performance, security, and reliability.

- Routing: Network automation can help manage routing protocols and route redistribution, ensuring optimal path selection and minimizing network congestion. Python libraries like Exscript or Netmiko can be used to automate routing configurations and updates.

- Switching: Automation can simplify the management of VLANs, spanning tree protocols, and other switching-related configurations. This can help prevent misconfigurations that may lead to network loops or other issues.

- Security: Network automation can help enforce security policies, such as Access Control Lists (ACLs), VPN configurations, and firewall rules. Automation ensures that security configurations are applied consistently and can quickly update them as needed.

- QoS: Quality of Service (QoS) management involves prioritizing network traffic based on its type or source. Automating QoS configurations ensures that critical applications and services receive the necessary bandwidth and minimizes latency.

Configuration Management

Configuration management is a critical facet of network administration. It involves maintaining a standard configuration for network devices and applying changes as per requirements. Network automation can significantly enhance configuration management in several ways. Firstly, it ensures consistency across devices, reducing discrepancies and errors. Secondly, it simplifies mass configurations, saving time and resources. Thirdly, it provides the capability to revert to previous configurations when required, improving network stability. Lastly, automation supports auditing and compliance by maintaining detailed logs of configuration changes, thus fostering accountability and transparency.

Network automation can improve configuration management by:

- Standardizing configurations: By deploying standardized configurations, you can ensure that devices follow best practices, minimizing the risk of configuration-related issues.

- Change tracking: Automation tools can track and log configuration changes, allowing administrators to identify the cause of issues and roll back changes if necessary.

- Validation and compliance: Network automation can help validate configurations against predefined rules or standards, ensuring that devices adhere to organizational policies and industry best practices.

- Version control: By integrating network automation with version control systems like Git, you can keep a history of configuration changes, making it easier to track and manage different versions.

By incorporating automation into network devices, services, and configuration management, you can streamline operations, reduce human error, and improve overall network performance and security. Python, along with its libraries and frameworks, serves as a powerful tool to automate these tasks, making it an invaluable asset for network administrators.

Netmiko and Paramiko libraries

Paramiko and Netmiko are popular Python libraries used for automating network tasks, particularly for establishing and managing SSH connections to network devices. Let us learn about each of these libraries, their essential features, and how to install them in your existing Python environment.

About Paramiko

Paramiko is a versatile Python library designed to facilitate the implementation of the SSHv2 protocol, which is integral for establishing secure remote connections to network devices. This library allows users to execute commands and transfer files securely over these remote connections. Additionally, Paramiko offers support for the SFTP protocol, which is a secure, reliable method of transferring files between local and remote systems. Its robust features and emphasis on security make Paramiko an essential tool to automate a range of tasks while ensuring the integrity and confidentiality of data during transmission.

Some essential features of Paramiko include:

- Pure Python implementation of SSHv2: Paramiko is written entirely in Python, making it compatible with a wide range of systems without requiring additional dependencies.

- Supports key-based and password-based authentication: Paramiko allows for both public key and password-based authentication methods, providing flexibility in how you secure your connections.

- Provides an API for creating custom SSH clients and servers: With Paramiko, you can develop your own SSH-based applications, such as custom clients or servers, to suit your specific requirements.

Installing Paramiko

To install Paramiko, you can use the pip package manager. Open a terminal or command prompt and run the following command:

```
pip install paramiko
```

About Netmiko

Netmiko is a versatile Python library developed on the Paramiko framework, designed to streamline the process of connecting to and automating a variety of network devices over Secure Shell (SSH). It provides robust, higher-level abstractions and functionalities that simplify the complexities of managing connections, dispatching commands, and handling responses from a diverse set of network devices.

Some essential features of Netmiko include:

- Multi-vendor support: Netmiko supports a wide range of network devices from different vendors, including Cisco, Juniper, Arista, HP, and more, making it a versatile library for managing diverse network environments.

- Connection management: Netmiko handles the details of establishing, maintaining, and closing SSH connections to network devices, allowing you to focus on writing automation scripts.

- Output handling: Netmiko can parse and manipulate the output from network devices, making it easier to work with and process the data.

- Built-in error handling and recovery: Netmiko includes error-handling mechanisms that help recover from common issues such as timeouts, authentication failures, and unexpected device responses.

Installing Netmiko

To install Netmiko, use the pip package manager by running the following command in your terminal or command prompt:

```
pip install netmiko
```

By installing Paramiko and Netmiko, you'll have access to powerful tools for automating network tasks, managing SSH connections, and working with a wide range of network devices. These libraries will be instrumental in building efficient and reliable network automation scripts.

Managing VLANs

VLAN (Virtual Local Area Network) management involves creating, modifying, and deleting VLANs on network devices such as switches. VLANs are used to segment a network into smaller, isolated broadcast domains, improving performance and security. They allow devices within the same VLAN to communicate with each other, even if they are on different physical switches, while preventing communication with devices outside the VLAN.

In this demonstration, we will use the Netmiko library to manage VLANs on a Cisco switch. Netmiko simplifies the process of connecting to and automating network devices over SSH, making it a suitable choice for this task.

Below is a step-by-step walkthrough to managing VLANs using Netmiko:

Import Required libraries

In your Python script, import the necessary libraries:

```
from netmiko import ConnectHandler
```

Define Device Information

Specify the device details, such as device type, IP address, username, and password. Replace the placeholders with your device's actual information:

```
cisco_switch = {
```

```python
    'device_type': 'cisco_ios',
    'ip': '192.168.1.1',
    'username': 'your_username',
    'password': 'your_password',
}
```

Connect to Device

Establish an SSH connection to the switch using the ConnectHandler function:

```python
connection = ConnectHandler(**cisco_switch)
```

Create New VLAN

To create a new VLAN, define a function that sends the necessary commands to the switch:

```python
def create_vlan(connection, vlan_id, vlan_name):
    config_commands = [
        f'vlan {vlan_id}',
        f'name {vlan_name}',
    ]
    output = connection.send_config_set(config_commands)
    return output
```

Call the function with VLAN ID and name

```python
output = create_vlan(connection, 100, 'Test_VLAN')
print(output)
```

Delete VLAN

To delete a VLAN, define a function that sends the 'no vlan' command to the switch:

```python
def delete_vlan(connection, vlan_id):
    config_commands = [
```

```
        f'no vlan {vlan_id}',
    ]
    output = connection.send_config_set(config_commands)
    return output
```

Call this function with the VLAN ID you want to delete:

```
output = delete_vlan(connection, 100)
print(output)
```

Close the Connection

Finally, remember to close the SSH connection to the switch:

```
connection.disconnect()
```

By using Netmiko, you can easily manage VLANs on network devices, automating tasks like creating, modifying, and deleting VLANs. This can save time, reduce the risk of errors, and improve overall network performance and security.

Automating SSH connections

SSH (Secure Shell) is a cryptographic network protocol used to securely access and manage network devices and servers over an unsecured network. It provides a secure channel for executing commands, transferring files, and managing network devices remotely. Automating SSH connections can help streamline network management tasks and improve efficiency.

In this demonstration, we will use the Netmiko library to automate SSH connections to a network device. Netmiko is built on top of Paramiko and provides higher-level abstractions, making it easier to manage connections, send commands, and handle output from various network devices.

Below is a step-by-step walkthrough to automating SSH connections using Netmiko:

Define Device Information

Specify the device details, such as device type, IP address, username, and password. Replace the placeholders with your device's actual information:

```
network_device = {
    'device_type': 'cisco_ios',
    'ip': '192.168.1.1',
    'username': 'your_username',
    'password': 'your_password',
}
```

Connect to Device

Establish an SSH connection to the network device using the ConnectHandler function:

```
connection = ConnectHandler(**network_device)
```

Send Commands to Device

You can now send commands to the network device using the send_command method. For example, to retrieve the device's running configuration, use:

```
output = connection.send_command('show run')
print(output)
```

Send Configuration Commands

To send a set of configuration commands, use the send_config_set method. For example, to configure an interface, you can use the following code:

```
config_commands = [
    'interface GigabitEthernet0/1',
    'description Example Interface',
    'ip address 192.168.2.1 255.255.255.0',
    'no shutdown',
]
output = connection.send_config_set(config_commands)
print(output)
```

Close the Connection

Finally, remember to close the SSH connection to the network device:

```
connection.disconnect()
```

By using Netmiko, you can automate SSH connections to network devices, allowing you to execute commands and manage configurations programmatically. This can save time, reduce the risk of errors, and improve overall network management efficiency.

Executing Remote Commands

Remote commands are commands executed on a remote device, such as a server or network equipment, from a local machine. This is a common practice in network administration and management, as it allows administrators to manage devices without physically accessing them. Executing remote commands can help automate repetitive tasks, troubleshoot issues, and maintain network devices efficiently.

We will use the Netmiko library to demonstrate executing remote commands on a network device over an SSH connection. Netmiko simplifies the process of connecting to and automating network devices over SSH.

Below is a step-by-step walkthrough to executing remote commands using Netmiko:

Until connecting to the device, the steps remain the same as defined in the previous section.

Execute Remote Commands

Now that you have an SSH connection to the network device, you can execute remote commands using the send_command method. For example, to retrieve the device's hostname, use:

```
output = connection.send_command('show hostname')
print(output)
```

You can execute any command supported by the remote device using the send_command method. For example, to display the device's interface status, use:

```
output = connection.send_command('show interfaces status')
```

```
print(output)
```

Close the Connection

Finally, remember to close the SSH connection to the network device:

```
connection.disconnect()
```

By using Netmiko, you can execute remote commands on network devices over an SSH connection, allowing you to manage devices remotely, automate tasks, and troubleshoot issues efficiently.

Retrieving and Modifying Device Configuration

Retrieving and modifying network device configurations is an essential task for network administrators. By automating these tasks, you can save time, minimize human error, and maintain consistency across your network infrastructure. In this demonstration, we'll continue using the Netmiko library to retrieve and modify configurations on a Cisco network device over an SSH connection.

Below is a step-by-step walkthrough to retrieving and modifying network device configurations using Netmiko:

Until connecting to the device, the steps remain the same as defined in the previous section.

Retrieve the Running Configuration

To retrieve the running configuration from the network device, use the send_command method with the 'show run' command:

```
running_config = connection.send_command('show run')
print(running_config)
```

Modify the Configuration

To modify the configuration, use the send_config_set method with a list of configuration commands. For example, to configure an interface with a description, IP address, and enable it, use the following code:

```
config_commands = [
    'interface GigabitEthernet0/1',
    'description Example Interface',
    'ip address 192.168.2.1 255.255.255.0',
    'no shutdown',
]
output = connection.send_config_set(config_commands)
print(output)
```

Save the Configuration

To save the modified configuration to the startup configuration, so it persists across device reboots, use the save_config method:

```
output = connection.save_config()
print(output)
```

Close the Connection

Finally, remember to close the SSH connection to the network device:

```
connection.disconnect()
```

By using Netmiko, you can efficiently retrieve and modify network device configurations over an SSH connection, streamlining network administration tasks and improving the overall management of your network infrastructure.

Updating Device Firmware

Updating device firmware is a critical task in maintaining the health and security of your network infrastructure. However, each vendor and even different models within the same vendor can have very different processes for updating firmware.

Let us take a look at a general process for updating firmware on a network device using Python and some helpful libraries such as paramiko for SSH connection and scp for secure file transfer.

Download the Firmware

The first step is to download the new firmware version from the vendor's official website. Make sure to download the correct firmware version for your specific device model.

Upload Firmware to the Device

Once you have the new firmware, you need to upload it to the network device. This is usually done via Secure Copy Protocol (SCP). You can use the scp Python library to automate this task.

Using SCP

The given below is an example of how to use scp in Python to upload a file:

```python
from paramiko import SSHClient
from scp import SCPClient

ssh = SSHClient()
ssh.load_system_host_keys()
ssh.connect('hostname', username='user', password='passwd')

# SCPCLient takes a paramiko transport as an argument
with SCPClient(ssh.get_transport()) as scp:
    scp.put('test.txt', 'test2.txt')  # Copy test.txt to test2.txt
```

In the above sample program, replace 'hostname', 'user', and 'passwd' with your device's hostname (or IP address) and your SSH credentials. Also, replace 'test.txt' with the path to the firmware file on your local system, and 'test2.txt' with the desired location and filename on the remote system.

Install the Firmware

After the firmware file is uploaded to the device, you need to install it. This usually involves running specific commands on the device via SSH.

The given below is an example of how to use paramiko to execute commands on a remote device:

```
from paramiko import SSHClient

ssh = SSHClient()
ssh.load_system_host_keys()
ssh.connect('hostname', username='user', password='passwd')

stdin, stdout, stderr = ssh.exec_command("command to install firmware")
```

In the above snippet, replace 'hostname', 'user', and 'passwd' with your device's hostname (or IP address) and your SSH credentials. Replace "command to install firmware" with the specific command(s) required to install the firmware on your device.

Reboot the Device

After the firmware is installed, you typically need to reboot the device for the changes to take effect. This can usually be done by executing a reboot command over SSH, similar to the firmware installation step above.

Verify the Update

Finally, once the device has rebooted, you should verify that the firmware update was successful. This can usually be done by logging into the device and checking the firmware version. This can also be automated using paramiko to run the appropriate command and retrieve the output.

Remember that updating firmware can cause the device to become unavailable for a period of time and may cause disruptions in your network. Always plan firmware updates carefully and consider updating in a maintenance window when the network usage is low.

Summary

In this chapter, we took a deep dive into the world of network automation, exploring how Python and its libraries such as Paramiko and Netmiko can be used to automate repetitive and complex tasks in network administration. We started with the basic concepts of network automation, including the reasons for its increasing importance in modern network management and its key advantages such as increased speed, efficiency, and accuracy.

We then moved on to a detailed discussion on managing network devices, services, and configurations. We demonstrated how Python libraries like Paramiko and Netmiko can be used to automate tasks such as managing VLANs, establishing SSH connections, and executing remote commands. We showed how to retrieve and modify network device configurations using Netmiko, which offers a simplified way of interacting with network devices over SSH. This not only enables rapid deployment and troubleshooting but also ensures consistency across the network infrastructure.

Lastly, we explored the process of updating network device firmware using Python. We emphasized the importance of careful planning and execution of firmware updates to minimize network disruption. The chapter concluded with examples of common socket errors that can occur during network automation tasks and strategies for handling these errors using Python.

Chapter 5: Network Monitoring and Analysis

Overview of Network Monitoring & Analysis

Network monitoring and analysis form a crucial part of the job for network administrators. They are essential for maintaining optimal network performance, ensuring network security, and minimizing downtime. Let us explore these in detail:

What is Network Monitoring?

Network monitoring is the practice of consistently overseeing a computer network for any failures or discrepancies. It is an essential IT process where all networking components like routers, switches, firewalls, servers, and VMs are monitored for fault and performance and evaluated continuously to maintain and optimize their availability. Effective network monitoring can lead to significant cost savings by preventing network disruptions and reducing downtime.

What is Network Analysis?

Network analysis refers to the method of inspecting, reviewing, and recording information about a network's data to identify trends or patterns. It helps in the diagnosis of problems and in the design of network updates. Network analysis can give insights into network performance, allowing network administrators to understand how data is being transmitted and where bottlenecks may occur.

Types of Network Monitoring

There are several types of network monitoring, each focusing on a different aspect of the network:

Performance Monitoring: This involves monitoring the performance of network elements such as routers, switches, and servers to ensure they are operating correctly and efficiently.

Fault Monitoring: This involves checking network elements for errors or failures. When a fault is detected, the system can alert network administrators so that they can rectify the problem.

Security Monitoring: This involves monitoring the network for suspicious activities or attacks. If an attack is detected, the system can alert network administrators or even take steps to mitigate the attack.

Traffic Monitoring: This involves monitoring the flow of data within the network. This can help administrators understand how network resources are being used and identify any potential bottlenecks.

Network Analysis Tools

Network administrators use a variety of tools for network analysis. These tools can provide information on a range of factors, including packet loss, throughput levels, and network latency. They can also identify which devices are connected to the network and how they are communicating with each other. Some commonly used network analysis tools include Wireshark, Ping, and traceroute.

Python in Network Monitoring and Analysis

Python, with its robust set of libraries and packages, is an ideal language for network monitoring and analysis. It has libraries like Scapy for packet analysis, Nmap for network scanning, and PySNMP for interacting with devices using the Simple Network Management Protocol (SNMP). These tools allow you to create powerful, customized network monitoring and analysis solutions.

In the following sections, we will explore in more detail how Python can be used for SNMP, network traffic monitoring, network performance monitoring, and troubleshooting.

Exploring SNMP and its Python library

Simple Network Management Protocol

Simple Network Management Protocol (SNMP) is a popular protocol used for managing devices in IP networks. It allows for the exchange of information between network devices, making it possible to manage and monitor these devices remotely. SNMP is used for gathering information from various network devices, such as servers, routers, switches, printers, and more, across an Internet Protocol (IP) network.

SNMP works by sending protocol data units (PDUs) to different parts of a network. SNMP-compliant devices, known as agents, store data about themselves in Management Information Bases (MIBs) and return this data to the SNMP requesters.

There are three versions of SNMP: SNMPv1, SNMPv2c, and SNMPv3. SNMPv1 is the original version of the protocol. SNMPv2c is an update that includes additional protocol operations. SNMPv3 adds security and remote configuration capabilities to the previous versions.

PySNMP Overview

PySNMP is a versatile and comprehensive Python library designed to facilitate the creation of SNMP applications. It supports all versions of the SNMP protocol (SNMPv1, SNMPv2c, and SNMPv3), making it a valuable tool for building network management software for both SNMP managers and agents. PySNMP enables users to perform various SNMP operations, such as retrieving and manipulating data from SNMP-enabled devices, allowing network administrators to monitor and manage network devices effectively.

Installing PySNMP

To get started with PySNMP, you first need to install it. You can do so using pip, which is the package installer for Python. Following are the steps to install PySNMP:

Open your command prompt (CMD) or terminal.

Type the following command and press Enter:

```
pip install pysnmp
```

Wait for the installation process to complete.

Once PySNMP is installed, you can import it into your Python scripts using the following line of code:

```
from pysnmp.hlapi import *
```

In the upcoming sections, we'll explore how to use PySNMP to perform SNMP operations such as GET, SET, and WALK, which allow you to retrieve, modify, and traverse the data stored in an SNMP agent's MIBs respectively.

SNMP Operations using PySNMP

let us dive into the main SNMP operations - GET, SET, and WALK. Each of these operations serves a different purpose in an SNMP-based network management system.

GET Operation

The GET operation is used to retrieve the value of a specific variable. The manager sends a GET request to an agent to retrieve the value of one or more specified object instances.

When the agent receives the GET request, it will respond with the values.

Below is an example of a GET operation that retrieves the sysDescr object, which contains a description of the system:

```python
from pysnmp.hlapi import *

iterator = getCmd(
    SnmpEngine(),
    CommunityData('public'),
    UdpTransportTarget(('demo.snmplabs.com', 161)),
    ContextData(),
    ObjectType(ObjectIdentity('SNMPv2-MIB', 'sysDescr', 0))
)

errorIndication, errorStatus, errorIndex, varBinds = next(iterator)

if errorIndication:
    print(errorIndication)
elif errorStatus:
    print('%s at %s' % (errorStatus.prettyPrint(), errorIndex and
varBinds[int(errorIndex) - 1][0] or '?'))
else:
    for varBind in varBinds:
        print(' = '.join([x.prettyPrint() for x in varBind]))
```

SET Operation

The SET operation is used to assign the value to a specific variable on the device. The manager sends a SET request to change the value of an object instance in the agent's MIB. This allows the manager to control the behavior of the agent.

Below is an example of a SET operation that changes the value of the sysContact object, which contains the contact information for the person responsible for the system:

```python
from pysnmp.hlapi import *

iterator = setCmd(
    SnmpEngine(),
    CommunityData('public'),
    UdpTransportTarget(('demo.snmplabs.com', 161)),
    ContextData(),
    ObjectType(ObjectIdentity('SNMPv2-MIB', 'sysContact', 0),
'test@example.com')
)

errorIndication, errorStatus, errorIndex, varBinds = next(iterator)

if errorIndication:
    print(errorIndication)
elif errorStatus:
    print('%s at %s' % (errorStatus.prettyPrint(), errorIndex and
varBinds[int(errorIndex) - 1][0] or '?'))
else:
    for varBind in varBinds:
        print(' = '.join([x.prettyPrint() for x in varBind]))
```

<u>WALK Operation</u>

The WALK operation is used to retrieve multiple object instances in a single operation. A WALK request starts at a specified object instance and then retrieves the next object instance in the MIB until there are no more instances left. This operation is useful for exploring what data is available on an SNMP agent.

Below is an example of a WALK operation that retrieves all object instances under the system object:

```python
from pysnmp.hlapi import *

for (errorIndication, errorStatus, errorIndex, varBinds) in nextCmd(
```

```python
    SnmpEngine(),
    CommunityData('public'),
    UdpTransportTarget(('demo.snmplabs.com', 161)),
    ContextData(),
    ObjectType(ObjectIdentity('SNMPv2-MIB', 'system')),
    lexicographicMode=False
):
    if errorIndication:
        print(errorIndication)
        break
    elif errorStatus:
        print('%s at %s' % (errorStatus.prettyPrint(), errorIndex and
varBinds[int(errorIndex) - 1][0] or '?'))
        break
    else:
        for varBind in varBinds:
            print(' = '.join([x.prettyPrint() for x in varBind]))
```

This script performs a WALK operation starting at the 'system' object in the SNMPv2-MIB. The 'lexicographicMode=False' argument stops the walk when it reaches an object outside the 'system' subtree. The script prints each object instance it retrieves. Keep in mind that these examples are using the 'demo.snmplabs.com' target, which is a public SNMP test server. You would replace this with the address of your own SNMP agent, and you would also replace 'public' with your own community string. The community string is a form of password that controls access to the SNMP agent's MIB. 'Public' is a common default, but in a real-world situation, you should use a more secure community string.

These PySNMP examples show how you can use Python to interact with SNMP. Python and SNMP together provide a powerful tool for network management, allowing you to automate many tasks that would be time-consuming to perform manually.

SNMP TRAP

PySNMP offers advanced capabilities beyond the basic GET, SET, and WALK operations. For example, you can use PySNMP to send SNMP TRAPs or INFORMs, which are unsolicited messages from an SNMP agent to an SNMP manager. This can be useful for notifying the manager of important events or changes in the network.

Below is an example of how to send an SNMP TRAP using PySNMP:

```python
from pysnmp.hlapi import *

sendNotification(
    SnmpEngine(),
    CommunityData('public'),
    UdpTransportTarget(('demo.snmplabs.com', 162)),
    ContextData(),
    'trap',
    NotificationType(ObjectIdentity('SNMPv2-MIB', 'coldStart'))
)
```

This script sends a coldStart trap to the manager, indicating that the SNMP agent has reinitialized itself.

GET Operation using SNMPv3

Another advanced capability of PySNMP is its support for SNMPv3, which offers enhanced security features compared to the earlier versions of SNMP. SNMPv3 supports user authentication and encryption of SNMP messages, which can protect against unauthorized access and interception of SNMP traffic.

Below is an example of how to perform a GET operation using SNMPv3 with authentication and privacy (encryption):

```python
from pysnmp.hlapi import *

iterator = getCmd(
    SnmpEngine(),
    UsmUserData('user', 'authkey', 'privkey',
authProtocol=usmHMACSHAAuthProtocol,
privProtocol=usmAesCfb128Protocol),
    UdpTransportTarget(('demo.snmplabs.com', 161)),
    ContextData(),
```

```python
    ObjectType(ObjectIdentity('SNMPv2-MIB', 'sysDescr', 0))
)

errorIndication, errorStatus, errorIndex, varBinds = next(iterator)

if errorIndication:
    print(errorIndication)
elif errorStatus:
    print('%s at %s' % (errorStatus.prettyPrint(), errorIndex and
varBinds[int(errorIndex) - 1][0] or '?'))
else:
    for varBind in varBinds:
        print(' = '.join([x.prettyPrint() for x in varBind]))
```

In this script, the UsmUserData object is used to specify the SNMPv3 user and the authentication and privacy keys. The authProtocol argument is used to specify the authentication protocol, and the privProtocol argument is used to specify the privacy protocol.

Network Traffic Monitoring

Network traffic monitoring is a critical aspect of network management. It allows network administrators to understand the volume and type of traffic on their network, identify patterns, troubleshoot issues, and plan for future capacity needs.

The first step in network traffic monitoring is to identify what you want to measure. Common metrics include:

- Bandwidth Usage: This is the amount of data transferred over your network per unit of time. High bandwidth usage can slow down your network and affect performance.

- Packet Loss: This is the number of packets that fail to reach their destination. Packet loss can cause interruptions in network services and degrade the quality of voice and video calls.

- Latency: This is the amount of time it takes for a packet to travel from its source to its destination. High latency can cause delays in data transmission and affect the performance of real-time applications.

- Jitter: This is the variation in latency over time. High jitter can cause issues with voice and video calls, as well as with some types of online games.

- Throughput: This is the rate at which data is successfully delivered over a network connection. Low throughput can slow down file transfers and other data-intensive tasks.

Python is an excellent tool for network traffic monitoring due to its flexibility and the wide range of libraries available for networking tasks. For example, you can use the pcapy library to capture packets and the dpkt library to parse them.

Below is an example of a simple Python script that captures packets and prints out their source and destination IP addresses:

```python
import pcapy
from dpkt import ethernet, ip

def print_packet(hdr, data):
    packet = ethernet.Ethernet(data)
    if isinstance(packet.data, ip.IP):
        print("Source: %s -> Destination: %s" % (packet.data.src, packet.data.dst))

capture = pcapy.open_live("eth0", 65536, 1, 0)
capture.loop(0, print_packet)
```

In this script, pcapy.open_live is used to start packet capture on the "eth0" network interface. The capture.loop function is then used to process each captured packet with the print_packet function.

The print_packet function parses each packet as an Ethernet frame using dpkt.ethernet.Ethernet, then checks if the frame's payload is an IP packet. If it is, the function prints out the source and destination IP addresses of the packet. While this script provides a simple program of network traffic monitoring, real-world monitoring tasks can be much more complex. For example, you might want to aggregate statistics over time, filter for specific types of traffic, or generate alerts based on certain conditions.

Python's flexibility and the power of its networking libraries allow you to customize your monitoring scripts to fit your specific needs. You can also integrate Python scripts with other network monitoring tools to create a comprehensive monitoring solution. In addition to monitoring network traffic, Python can also be used to analyze network traffic. This involves examining captured network traffic to understand its characteristics and behavior. Network traffic analysis can help you identify trends, detect anomalies, and investigate security incidents.

For example, you might use Python to analyze network traffic for signs of a distributed denial-of-service (DDoS) attack, such as a sudden increase in traffic volume or a large number of packets from a single source. Python's data analysis libraries, such as pandas and matplotlib, can be helpful for this kind of analysis.

Below is an example of a Python script that captures packets and analyzes them to identify potential DDoS attacks:

```python
import pcapy
from dpkt import ethernet, ip
import pandas as pd


# Initialize a DataFrame to store packet data
df = pd.DataFrame

columns=['timestamp', 'source', 'destination'])

def capture_packet(hdr, data):
    timestamp = hdr.getts()[0]
    packet = ethernet.Ethernet(data)
    if isinstance(packet.data, ip.IP):
        source = packet.data.src
        destination = packet.data.dst
        df.loc[len(df)] = [timestamp, source, destination]

capture = pcapy.open_live("eth0", 65536, 1, 0)
capture.loop(0, capture_packet)
```

```python
# Now that we have our data, we can start analyzing it.
# Let us look for any IP addresses that are sending an unusually high number of
packets.

source_counts = df['source'].value_counts()
ddos_sources = source_counts[source_counts > 1000]  # This threshold may
need to be adjusted.

if not ddos_sources.empty:
    print("Potential DDoS attack detected from the following IP addresses:")
    print(ddos_sources)
```

This script extends the previous example by storing packet data in a pandas DataFrame
and using this to analyze the traffic. The capture_packet function captures each packet's
timestamp and source and destination IP addresses, and adds these to the DataFrame. After
capturing the data, the script counts the number of packets from each source IP address.
If it finds any IP addresses that have sent more than a certain number of packets (in this
case, 1000), it prints these out as potential DDoS attackers.

Measuring Network Performance

The process of measuring network performance characteristics such as bandwidth, packet
loss, latency, jitter, and throughput can be a complex task and often requires the use of
specialized network measurement tools. In Python, you can use existing libraries and
system utilities to measure some of these metrics. Following are some simple programs of
how you might do this:

Bandwidth Usage

Python can use the psutil library to get network IO statistics. Below is a basic script:

```python
import psutil
import time

def print_network_io():
    io1 = psutil.net_io_counters()
```

```python
    time.sleep(1)
    io2 = psutil.net_io_counters()
    sent = io2.bytes_sent - io1.bytes_sent
    recv = io2.bytes_recv - io1.bytes_recv
    print('Sent: {:0.2f} KB'.format(sent / 1024))
    print('Received: {:0.2f} KB'.format(recv / 1024))


print_network_io()
```

This script shows the amount of data sent and received over the network in the past second.

Packet Loss

Python can use the ping3 library to send ICMP echo requests and measure packet loss. Below is a basic script:

```python
from ping3 import ping, verbose_ping


def packet_loss(destination, count=4):
    return verbose_ping(destination, count, timeout=1)


print(packet_loss('8.8.8.8'))
```

This script pings a given IP address (in this case, 8.8.8.8) and returns the packet loss percentage.

Latency:

Python can use the ping3 library to measure latency. Below is a basic script:

```python
from ping3 import ping


def latency(destination):
    return ping(destination)
```

```python
print(latency('8.8.8.8'))
```

This script pings a given IP address and returns the round-trip time in milliseconds.

Jitter

Python can use the ping3 library to measure jitter. Below is a basic script:

```python
from ping3 import ping
import numpy as np

def jitter(destination, count=4):
    delays = [ping(destination) for _ in range(count)]
    return np.std(delays)

print(jitter('8.8.8.8'))
```

This script sends several ICMP echo requests to a given IP address and calculates the standard deviation of the round-trip times.

Throughput

Measuring throughput can be complex, depending on the specific requirements. However, a simple way is to measure the amount of data that can be sent to a server in a given amount of time. This would typically involve setting up a server to receive the data and a client to send it. This script is an example of how you could measure throughput:

```python
import time
import socket

def measure_throughput(server_ip, server_port, duration):
    client_socket = socket.socket(socket.AF_INET, socket.SOCK_STREAM)
    client_socket.connect((server_ip, server_port))
    start = time.time()
    data = b'x' * 1024  # 1 KB of data
    while time.time() - start < duration:
```

```python
    client_socket.send(data)
end = time.time()
client_socket.close()
throughput = 1024 * duration / (end - start)
print(f'Throughput: {throughput} KB/s')
```

Analyzing Network Performance

Analyzing network performance involves interpreting data collected from network monitoring tools to evaluate the efficiency and effectiveness of the network. In Python, you can use libraries such as Matplotlib, Pandas, and Numpy to analyze and visualize network performance data.

The given below is a simplified example of how you might analyze network performance data using Python. In the below example, we'll assume that we have a CSV file containing network latency data that we've collected, and we want to analyze this data to identify any trends or issues.

The CSV file (named latency_data.csv) has the following format:

time	latency
1620321000	25.6
1620321060	27.1
1620321120	26.4

Load the Data

We can use the pandas library to load this data into a DataFrame, which is a type of data structure provided by pandas that makes it easy to analyze structured data.

```python
import pandas as pd

# Load the CSV data into a pandas DataFrame
df = pd.read_csv('latency_data.csv')
```

```python
# Convert the 'time' column to datetime format
df['time'] = pd.to_datetime(df['time'], unit='s')


# Set the 'time' column as the index
df.set_index('time', inplace=True)


print(df.head())
```

Analyze the Data

Once the data is loaded into a DataFrame, we can use the various functions provided by pandas to analyze the data. For example, we can calculate the average latency, the maximum latency, and the minimum latency.

```python
# Calculate the average latency
avg_latency = df['latency'].mean()
print(f'Average latency: {avg_latency} ms')

# Calculate the maximum latency
max_latency = df['latency'].max()
print(f'Maximum latency: {max_latency} ms')

# Calculate the minimum latency
min_latency = df['latency'].min()
print(f'Minimum latency: {min_latency} ms')
```

Visualize the Data

We can use the Matplotlib library to create a plot of the latency data, which can help us identify any trends or patterns.

```python
import matplotlib.pyplot as plt
```

```python
# Create a plot of the latency data
plt.figure(figsize=(10, 6))
plt.plot(df.index, df['latency'], label='Latency')
plt.xlabel('Time')
plt.ylabel('Latency (ms)')
plt.title('Network Latency Over Time')
plt.legend()
plt.grid(True)
plt.show()
```

This script will create a line plot of the network latency over time, which can help you visualize how the latency is changing and identify any trends or issues.

Summary

In Chapter 5, we embarked on the journey of network monitoring and analysis, a crucial aspect of network management that helps identify potential issues and maintain the overall health of the network. Starting with Simple Network Management Protocol (SNMP), we understood its significance in the management of networked devices. We explored the Python library PySNMP, which simplifies SNMP operations, allowing us to retrieve and manipulate data from SNMP-enabled devices. From basic to modern usage, we practiced SNMP operations, discovering the versatility of this protocol.

Subsequently, we dived into the world of network traffic monitoring, learning about its various indicators like bandwidth usage, packet loss, latency, jitter, and throughput. We harnessed the power of Python libraries like psutil and scapy to create scripts that capture live network traffic data and analyze it, learning how to measure these indicators practically. We discussed how to calculate the bandwidth usage, demonstrated how to measure packet loss, and saw how to evaluate latency, jitter, and throughput. This part of the chapter provided a comprehensive understanding of network traffic monitoring and performance analysis.

Finally, we explored the analysis of network performance, where we utilized Python's data analysis libraries like pandas and Matplotlib. We discussed how to load network data, conduct basic analysis, and visualize the results. This analysis can identify trends and anomalies that might indicate network issues. Thus, in this chapter, we learned how Python aids in automating and simplifying network monitoring and analysis, demonstrating its vast capabilities in the realm of network management.

CHAPTER 6: NETWORK SECURITY AND PYTHON

Network Security Concepts

As networks continue to expand and evolve, the demand for network security has never been more significant. With the growing number of connected devices and the increasing reliance on digital systems, networks are becoming more vulnerable to various threats. Cybercriminals are constantly developing new techniques to exploit network vulnerabilities and gain unauthorized access to sensitive information. As a result, it is crucial to understand the importance of network security and implement effective strategies to protect the integrity, confidentiality, and availability of network resources.

Network security encompasses a wide range of measures and strategies aimed at safeguarding network infrastructure and data from unauthorized access, misuse, modification, or destruction. The primary objectives of network security are to protect the network from external threats, such as hackers and malware, and internal threats, like unauthorized access and data leaks. To achieve these objectives, network security professionals utilize a combination of hardware, software, policies, and best practices to create a layered defense that can adapt to the ever-changing threat landscape.

Some of the key concepts in network security include:

- Confidentiality: Ensuring that sensitive information is only accessible to authorized individuals and is protected from unauthorized access.

- Integrity: Maintaining the accuracy and consistency of data and ensuring it remains unaltered during storage, transmission, or processing.

- Availability: Ensuring that network resources and services are accessible to authorized users when needed, without any significant disruptions or downtime.

- Authentication: Verifying the identity of users, devices, or systems attempting to access network resources.

- Authorization: Defining and managing the permissions and access rights of users, devices, or systems within a network.

- Non-repudiation: Ensuring that an action, such as a data transfer or a command, cannot be denied by the party responsible for it.

As we proceed through this chapter, we will delve deeper into these concepts and explore various network security measures, such as firewalls, intrusion detection and prevention systems, virtual private networks, and access control. We will also discuss how Python can be used to implement and enhance network security practices, demonstrating its applicability in this critical area of network management.

Setting up Firewall

Setting up a firewall involves defining a set of rules to control incoming and outgoing network traffic based on the IP address, port number, and protocol. Below is a general outline of the process using Python's iptables module, which provides an interface to the Linux iptables utility. Note that this module works only on Linux systems and requires superuser privileges.

Install Python iptables Module

You can install the Python iptables module using pip:

```
pip install python-iptables
```

Import iptables Module

In your Python script, import the iptables module:

```
import iptables
```

Define Rule

An iptables rule is defined as an instance of the Rule class. You can specify the source and destination IP addresses, the protocol, and the action to be taken when a packet matches the rule:

```
rule = iptables.Rule()
rule.src = "10.0.0.1"
rule.dst = "10.0.0.2"
rule.protocol = "tcp"
rule.target = "ACCEPT"
```

Add Rule to Chain

A chain is a list of rules that are checked in order. If a packet matches a rule, the action specified by the rule's target is taken. You can add your rule to the INPUT chain, which processes incoming packets:

```
chain = iptables.Table(iptables.Table.FILTER).get_chain("INPUT")
chain.insert_rule(rule)
```

This Python script adds a rule to the INPUT chain of the filter table, which accepts all TCP packets coming from 10.0.0.1 to 10.0.0.2.

One thing to be cautious about is that modifying iptables rules can disrupt network connectivity, so you should always ensure that you have another way to access the system before making changes. Another thing is that iptables rules are not persistent across reboots, so you need to use a service like iptables-persistent or a tool like firewalld or ufw to save and reload rules automatically. And most important thing is that misconfiguration can lead to unexpected behavior, including loss of network connectivity.

Scanning and Analyzing Network Vulnerability

Network vulnerability scanning is an essential process in preserving network security, often conducted as part of routine network maintenance. This process involves a comprehensive assessment of your network, identifying potential weak points or vulnerabilities that could be exploited by malicious entities. These vulnerabilities could range from outdated software and misconfigured network devices to known exploits that, when leveraged, could allow unauthorized access to your network. Regular vulnerability scanning helps to ensure that these weak points are identified and fixed promptly, thereby reducing the risk of a successful cyber attack.

Python's nmap library is a widely used tool for performing network vulnerability scans. Nmap, which stands for Network Mapper, is an open-source tool designed for network discovery and security auditing. It's a powerful and flexible tool that can send custom packets and analyze the responses to discover hosts and services on a computer network. Using nmap in Python allows for the integration of its robust functionality directly into Python scripts, making it possible to automate and customize the scanning process. Furthermore, it provides a user-friendly interface for detailed network analysis, making it a valuable tool in any network administrator's toolkit.

Install Python nmap Module

You can install the Python nmap module using pip:

```
pip install python-nmap
```

Import nmap Module

In your Python script, import the nmap module:

```
import nmap
```

Initialize PortScanner Class

The PortScanner class provides methods for network scanning. You can create an instance of this class:

```
nm = nmap.PortScanner()
```

Scan Range of IP Addresses

You can use the scan method to perform a network scan. For instance, the following code scans the IP addresses from 192.168.1.1 to 192.168.1.10:

```
nm.scan('192.168.1.1/24', '22-443')
```

The first argument specifies the range of IP addresses, and the second argument specifies the range of ports to scan. In the above snippet, the scanner checks whether ports 22 to 443 are open on any devices in the IP range.

Analyze Results

The scan method returns a dictionary containing the results of the scan. You can examine this dictionary to identify open ports and potential vulnerabilities:

```
for host in nm.all_hosts():
    print('Host : %s (%s)' % (host, nm[host].hostname()))
    print('State : %s' % nm[host].state())
```

```python
for proto in nm[host].all_protocols():
    print('----------')
    print('Protocol : %s' % proto)

    lport = nm[host][proto].keys()
    for port in lport:
        print('port : %s\tstate : %s' % (port, nm[host][proto][port]['state']))
```

This code prints information about each host that was scanned, including the host's IP address, state (up or down), and the state of each port (open or closed).

It's crucial to underscore that scanning networks without explicit permission can lead to legal and ethical issues. Network scanning is a powerful tool, but like all tools, it must be used responsibly and ethically. Always ensure you have the required permissions before initiating any network scanning activities. Unauthorized scanning is considered intrusive and potentially harmful, equivalent to cyber trespassing. Moreover, vulnerability scanning is merely a single facet of a comprehensive network security strategy. While it helps identify potential weaknesses, it doesn't rectify them. Therefore, a robust security approach should include a patch management system to rectify the identified vulnerabilities effectively.

Secure Communication with SSL/TLS

Secure Socket Layer (SSL) and its successor, Transport Layer Security (TLS), are protocols used to establish a secure and encrypted connection between two systems. It can be a server connecting to another server or a client connecting to a server. SSL/TLS is most commonly used when a web browser needs to securely connect to a web server over the unsafe internet.

Python's ssl module, part of the standard library, provides a Pythonic interface to the OpenSSL library, which enables you to create secure connections. Below is a simple program of how you might establish a secure connection to a server using this module.

Import Socket and SSL Modules

You'll need the socket and ssl modules to establish a secure connection:

```python
import socket
import ssl
```

Create a Socket

Create a socket object using the socket.socket() function:

```
sock = socket.socket(socket.AF_INET, socket.SOCK_STREAM)
```

Wrap the Socket

Use the ssl.wrap_socket() function to wrap your socket with SSL/TLS:

```
wrappedSocket = ssl.wrap_socket(sock)
```

Connect to the Server

Use the connect() method to connect to the server you want to communicate with:

```
wrappedSocket.connect(('www.python.org', 443))
```

Send and Receive Data

Now you can send and receive data from the server using the send() and recv() methods:

```
wrappedSocket.send(b"GET / HTTP/1.1\r\nHost: www.python.org\r\n\r\n")
response = wrappedSocket.recv(4096)
```

Close the Connection

When you're done, use the close() method to close the connection:

```
wrappedSocket.close()
```

Remember to always verify the server's SSL certificate when establishing a secure connection. Failing to do so can make you vulnerable to man-in-the-middle attacks. You can use the ssl.get_server_certificate() function to get a server's certificate and then check if it's valid.

Intrusion Detection and Prevention

Intrusion Detection Systems (IDS) and Intrusion Prevention Systems (IPS) are vital components of network security. IDS systems monitor network traffic for suspicious activities and alert administrators about potential threats. IPS goes a step further, not only detecting potential threats but also taking action to prevent them.

One commonly used open-source network IDS is Snort, which uses a rule-driven language to analyze network traffic and alert on suspicious behavior. While Snort itself isn't Python-based, there are Python libraries that interact with Snort to enhance its capabilities.

Snortunsock, for instance, is a Python library that allows interaction with Snort's Unix Socket output plugin. This enables you to directly process alerts from Snort within your Python code, providing the ability to develop custom responses to detected intrusions.

However, building a full-fledged IDS/IPS in Python from scratch would be a monumental task, involving deep understanding of network protocols, potential vulnerabilities, and sophisticated data analysis techniques.

The following example gives a simple demonstration of how one might use Python to detect a potential intrusion by analyzing network traffic:

```python
import psutil

# Check all network connections
for conn in psutil.net_connections(kind='inet'):
    # If the connection is "listen" and the process is not "None"
    if conn.status == 'LISTEN' and conn.pid != None:
        # Fetch the process info using the process ID
        p = psutil.Process(conn.pid)
        print(f"{p.name()} is listening on port {conn.laddr.port} and the PID is {conn.pid}")
```

This script uses the psutil library to fetch all active network connections. If a connection is in a listening state, it fetches the process name using the process ID. In this way, you could monitor for unexpected or suspicious processes listening on your network, which may indicate a potential intrusion.

For more sophisticated intrusion detection and prevention, use Scapy or PyShark for crafting and interpreting network packets, which can be used to build more complex IDS/IPS systems. However, these are advanced topics and go beyond the basics of network security but I am going to give you a quick walkthrough to it in the next section.

Exploring Scapy

Scapy is a powerful Python library and interactive environment for handling and manipulating network packets. It can be used to construct, send, capture, and analyze network packets at various layers of the network stack. Scapy supports a wide range of protocols, and it offers a flexible and expressive API for defining and working with network data.

Below is a step-by-step walkthrough to using Scapy:

Installation

You can install Scapy using pip:

```
pip install scapy
```

Importing Scapy

Once installed, you can import Scapy into your Python script:

```
from scapy.all import *
```

Creating Packets

Scapy allows you to create network packets. Below is an example of creating an ICMP (Internet Control Message Protocol) packet:

```
packet = IP(dst="8.8.8.8") / ICMP()
```

Sending Packets

After creating a packet, you can send it using one of Scapy's send functions:

```
send(packet)
```

Capturing Packets

Scapy can also be used to capture network packets. Below is an example of capturing packets:

```
packets = sniff(count=10)
packets.summary()
```

Analyzing Packets

Once you've captured packets, you can analyze them. For instance, you can print details of each packet:

```
for packet in packets:
    print(packet.show())
```

Establishing VPNs

Creating a Virtual Private Network (VPN) involves complex protocols, encryption methodologies, and network routing aspects that are typically handled by specialized software and hardware solutions. It's not something you would generally do from scratch in Python, but rather you'd use existing VPN software (like OpenVPN, WireGuard, etc.) and then use Python to control or interact with that software if needed.

That being said, you can use Python to automate the process of setting up a VPN connection if the connection details are already known. This usually involves running system commands or interfacing with system libraries to establish the VPN connection.

VPN Connection using openVPN

Below is a simple example using the subprocess module to initiate a VPN connection on a Linux machine using OpenVPN:

```
import subprocess


# Define the command to start the VPN connection.
# This would typically involve running the OpenVPN command with appropriate
arguments,
```

# such as the path to a configuration file.
command = ["sudo", "openvpn", "--config", "/path/to/your/config.ovpn"]

# Use subprocess to run the command.
process = subprocess.Popen(command)

# The VPN connection will now be initiated.
# The Python script will not end until the VPN connection ends.
process.wait()

This is an absolute simple example, but it gives you an idea of how you can use Python to control other software on your system. If you're using a different VPN solution or a different operating system, the specifics would be different. Some VPN providers also offer API interfaces that you can interact with using Python, which might allow for more control over the VPN connection. However, this would depend on the specific VPN service being used.

It's also important to remember that using a VPN will affect all network traffic from your machine, not just the traffic from your Python script. If you only want to route specific network requests through a VPN, you might want to look into using a proxy server instead, which can be controlled on a per-request basis in Python using libraries like requests.

Summary

In this chapter, we have delved into the complex world of network security and how Python can be a useful tool in this domain. Beginning with understanding the vulnerability of networks and the demand for network security, we explored various aspects that contribute to the overall safety of a network. We dove into setting up firewalls, an integral part of a network that safeguards it from unauthorized access and malicious attacks. Python, with its diverse libraries, can aid in configuring and managing firewalls with a straightforward programming approach, making it less tedious and more efficient.

The essence of network security is not just about prevention but also about the detection and management of vulnerabilities. We have learned how to scan and analyze network vulnerabilities using Python libraries, which can help identify potential threats and weaknesses in the network. Additionally, we explored secure communication protocols like SSL/TLS and how to implement them using Python for encrypted and secure data transmission.

In the later part of the chapter, we introduced intrusion detection and prevention - crucial for maintaining the integrity of any network. Python's flexibility and robustness come into play here, offering various libraries and tools for network analysis and packet manipulation, such as Scapy. We also discussed VPNs, a widely-used method to secure network communication. Although creating a VPN involves complex protocols typically handled by specialized software, Python can automate the process of setting up a VPN connection, providing a seamless interface to control other system software. By the end of this chapter, you should have a thorough understanding of network security and how Python can be utilized effectively to ensure and enhance it.

Chapter 7: Working with APIs and Network Services

As our global society becomes increasingly interconnected, the role and responsibilities of Network Administrators have dramatically expanded, moving beyond merely managing physical devices and establishing connections. Today's Network Administrators are also expected to proficiently handle a broad array of network services, which often entail the manipulation and management of data and resources across diverse platforms and systems. This expanded role has been primarily facilitated by Application Programming Interfaces, or APIs. APIs serve as the vital connecting links between different software applications, allowing them to communicate and share information seamlessly. They enable network administrators to integrate, manage, and interact with various network services, making them an essential tool in contemporary network management. As a result, proficiency in using and understanding APIs is now a fundamental skill required for modern network administration.

Application Programming Interfaces (API)

APIs are sets of rules and protocols that allow different software applications to communicate with each other. They define the methods and data formats that a program can use to perform tasks, like requesting data or invoking operations, on another software service. APIs have become an integral part of modern network services, allowing them to be controlled programmatically instead of through manual intervention. This allows tasks to be automated and scaled, increasing efficiency and reducing the possibility of human error.

Network administrators typically interact with APIs on network devices, software-defined networks (SDNs), and cloud services. These APIs can provide access to a wide variety of functionality, from retrieving device status information to configuring network parameters or even provisioning new network services.

Take, for example, a cloud provider like Amazon Web Services (AWS). AWS provides APIs for almost every service they offer, from virtual servers (EC2) to storage (S3) to networking (VPC). A network administrator could use these APIs to automate the process of setting up a new virtual private network, provisioning servers, and configuring network access rules. They could also use the APIs to monitor the status of these services, receiving automatic updates when certain events occur, such as a server going down or a storage bucket becoming full.

Another example could be the use of APIs on network devices like switches, routers, or firewalls. Instead of having to manually log in to each device to check its status or change its configuration, a network administrator could use the device's API to perform these tasks programmatically. This becomes even more valuable in large networks with many devices, where manual management would be impractical. In Python, interacting with APIs is often done using the requests library, which simplifies the process of making HTTP requests. JSON (JavaScript Object Notation) is a common format for sending and receiving data through APIs, and Python has built-in support for JSON, making it easy to parse and generate JSON data.

APIs provide a means to automate and scale tasks that would be time-consuming or impractical to perform manually. Understanding how to use APIs, and how to work with them in Python, is a valuable skill for any network administrator. In the upcoming sections of this chapter, we will dive deeper into working with APIs in Python, exploring different types of APIs, and learning how to use them effectively in networking tasks.

Types of APIs

APIs are diverse and can be categorized based on their purposes, the protocols they use, and how they expose their functions. In the context of networking, network administrators often work with several types of APIs, including REST APIs, SOAP APIs, XML-RPC, JSON-RPC, and device-level APIs.

REST APIs (Representational State Transfer)

REST APIs (Representational State Transfer) represent the most prevalent type of API in contemporary usage, primarily due to their simplicity, scalability, and stateless nature. REST is an architectural style that enables the design of networked applications. REST APIs utilize HTTP methods such as GET, POST, PUT, DELETE, among others, to perform Create, Read, Update, and Delete (CRUD) operations on resources identified via URLs. The stateless characteristic of REST APIs means that each HTTP request should contain all the information needed for the server to process the request, without relying on information from previous requests. This stateless property makes REST APIs ideal for cloud-based applications, including network management tasks. For instance, a REST API could be used to retrieve the status of a network device, modify its configuration, or even delete the device from the network.

SOAP APIs (Simple Object Access Protocol)

SOAP APIs (Simple Object Access Protocol) represent another type of API, typically found in enterprise and legacy systems. SOAP is a protocol developed to facilitate the exchange of structured information in web services using XML. Unlike REST APIs, SOAP APIs can operate over various protocols such as HTTP, SMTP, FTP, and more, giving it a high degree of versatility. However, SOAP APIs are more complex and heavyweight compared to REST APIs, leading to their reduced prevalence in modern web services. Despite this, they are still integral in scenarios that require robust security, transactional reliability, and ACID compliance.

XML-RPC and JSON-RPC

XML-RPC and JSON-RPC are remote procedure call (RPC) APIs that use XML and JSON, respectively, to encode their data. Like SOAP, they allow for direct interactions between software across a network, but they are simpler and more lightweight. They represent a middle ground between the complexity of SOAP and the simplicity of REST, offering flexibility without an excessive overhead. XML-RPC and JSON-RPC are typically used in systems where performance and bandwidth are not major concerns, but where the ability to make method calls remotely is necessary.

Device-level APIs

Device-level APIs represent a category of APIs specific to network devices, such as routers, switches, and firewalls. These APIs enable network administrators to interact with the device programmatically, performing tasks like retrieving status information, altering configurations, and more. The specifics of these APIs can vary significantly depending on the manufacturer and model of the device. They typically provide a granular level of control over the device, allowing administrators to perform a range of tasks that would otherwise require manual interaction with the device. For instance, a device-level API could be used to retrieve the current status of a router, update its routing table, or reset the device to its factory settings.

In addition to these, there are also APIs specifically designed for networking tasks. For example, Cisco provides a range of APIs for interacting with their devices and services, including the NX-API for Nexus devices, the IOS XE REST API for Catalyst devices, and the APIC-EM API for managing networks.

In Python, these APIs can be accessed using various libraries. The requests library is commonly used for HTTP-based APIs (REST, SOAP, JSON-RPC), while specific libraries might be needed for other types of APIs.

In the next sections, we will delve into how to use these APIs in a practical context, with examples of common tasks a network administrator might perform.

Using Python to Interact with APIs

To interact with APIs in Python, the requests library is most commonly used. The requests library simplifies sending HTTP requests, which is the core of interacting with REST APIs. Below is how you can use it:

Tracking Network Usage using REST API

Let us start with a simple program of using the REST API. Suppose you're a network administrator for a company that uses an online service with a REST API to track network usage data. The API could have an endpoint like http://api.networktracker.com/usage

GET Request: To retrieve network usage data for a specific day, you might send a GET request to /usage/2022-05-01:

```python
import requests

response = requests.get('http://api.networktracker.com/usage/2022-05-01')
data = response.json()
print(data)
```

The requests.get function sends a GET request to the specified URL. The response.json() method parses the JSON response body and converts it into a Python data structure (usually a dictionary or a list).

POST Request: If you want to add a new record of network usage data, you might send a POST request to /usage with a JSON body containing the new data:

```python
import requests
import json

data = {
    'date': '2022-05-12',
    'usage': 1500
}

response = requests.post('http://api.networktracker.com/usage',
data=json.dumps(data))
print(response.status_code)
```

This code sends a POST request with a JSON body. The json.dumps function converts a Python dictionary into a JSON string.

Using APIs with Authentication: Most APIs require some form of authentication. A common method is to use API keys, which are sent as a header in each API request:

```python
import requests
import json

headers = {
    'Authorization': 'Bearer YOUR_API_KEY'
}

response = requests.get('http://api.networktracker.com/usage/2022-05-01',
headers=headers)
data = response.json()
print(data)
```

In this case, the headers dictionary contains an Authorization header with the value 'Bearer YOUR_API_KEY'. Replace YOUR_API_KEY with your actual API key.

Error Handling: It's also important to handle potential errors when making API requests. The response.raise_for_status() method can be used to throw an exception if the HTTP request returned an error status:

```python
import requests

try:
    response = requests.get('http://api.networktracker.com/usage/2022-05-01')
    response.raise_for_status()
except requests.exceptions.HTTPError as err:
    print(f"HTTP error occurred: {err}")
except requests.exceptions.RequestException as err:
    print(f"Error occurred: {err}")
else:
    data = response.json()
    print(data)
```

You can observe that python and the requests library make it quite straightforward to interact with APIs.

Using GitHub API

GitHub's API is RESTful and it provides access to a variety of data including repositories, users, issues, and more. Suppose you're a network administrator and you want to fetch the list of repositories of a user, and for each repository, you want to fetch the list of its contributors. This involves dealing with pagination and nested requests.

The GitHub API requires authentication for some endpoints, and even for public endpoints, it allows a higher rate limit for authenticated requests. Below is how to authenticate using a personal access token:

```python
import requests

headers = {
    'Authorization': 'token YOUR_GITHUB_TOKEN'
}
```

Now, let us fetch the list of repositories for a user:

```python
username = 'torvalds'  # Linux creator Linus Torvalds
response = requests.get(f'https://api.github.com/users/{username}/repos',
headers=headers)
response.raise_for_status()  # Check for errors

repos = response.json()  # Parse JSON response
```

For each repository, let us fetch the list of contributors:

```python
for repo in repos:
    repo_name = repo['name']
    response =
requests.get(f'https://api.github.com/repos/{username}/{repo_name}/contribut
ors', headers=headers)
```

```python
    response.raise_for_status()

    contributors = response.json()
    print(f"Repo: {repo_name}")
    print("Contributors:")
    for contributor in contributors:
        print(contributor['login'])
```

This code prints the list of contributors for each repository of the user.

When working with real-world APIs, always consider the rate limits. Most APIs have a limit on how many requests you can send in a certain time period. The GitHub API, for example, allows 60 unauthenticated requests per hour and 5000 authenticated requests per hour.

Automatic Network Services

With the knowledge of interacting with APIs using Python learned in the previous sections, you can now automate various network services that provide an API. This may include configuring routers or switches, monitoring network performance, analyzing network traffic, and more.

Let us consider the scenario of a network administrator in a company with a large number of switches and routers. These devices need to be monitored, and configurations need to be updated regularly.

Before automation, this task might involve logging into each device manually, checking its status, and making necessary configuration changes. This could take a lot of time and is prone to human error. With network automation, this process can be automated using Python and APIs provided by the network devices. For example, many modern network devices support NETCONF or RESTCONF APIs that allow you to manage the device programmatically.

Firstly, you need to understand the API documentation provided by the network device manufacturer. Once you are clear about the available endpoints and the data format, you can write Python scripts using the requests library to interact with the API.

Automating Configuration of Network Device

For example, to get the configuration of a network device, you may have to send a GET request to a specific URL:

```python
import requests

url = 'https://device_ip/api/config'
response = requests.get(url, auth=('username', 'password'))
config = response.json()


print(config)
```

This script fetches the configuration of the network device and prints it.

Now, suppose you want to change the configuration of a device. You might send a PUT or PATCH request to update the configuration:

```python
new_config = {...}  # New configuration

response = requests.put(url, json=new_config, auth=('username', 'password'))
response.raise_for_status()  # Check for errors
```

This script updates the configuration of the network device.

By writing such scripts and running them on a schedule or in response to certain events, you can automate the task of monitoring and managing network devices.

You can automate complex workflows involving multiple devices, integrate with other systems, and much more. The key is to understand the capabilities of the API and how to use Python to interact with it.

Automating DNS Management

For businesses with a large number of domains, managing DNS records can be time-consuming. Luckily, many DNS providers offer APIs that allow you to automate DNS management. For example, you can write a Python script that uses the API to add, update, or delete DNS records automatically.

Let us look at an example of using the Cloudflare API to manage DNS records:

```python
import requests


# Replace these with your actual Cloudflare account details
zone_id = 'your_zone_id'
auth_email = 'your_email@example.com'
auth_key = 'your_auth_key'


# API URL for managing DNS records
url = f'https://api.cloudflare.com/client/v4/zones/{zone_id}/dns_records'


headers = {
    'X-Auth-Email': auth_email,
    'X-Auth-Key': auth_key,
}


# Get all DNS records
response = requests.get(url, headers=headers)
records = response.json()


for record in records['result']:
    print(record['name'], record['content'])
```

The script above retrieves and prints all DNS records in a given Cloudflare zone. You can modify this script to add, update, or delete DNS records based on your needs.

Automating Network Monitoring

Network monitoring tools like Zabbix, Nagios, or Prometheus provide APIs that you can use to automate the monitoring process. For example, you can write a Python script that periodically fetches monitoring data and generates reports, or that sends alerts based on specific conditions.

Let us look at an example of using the Zabbix API to fetch monitoring data:

```python
import requests

url = 'http://your_zabbix_server/zabbix/api_jsonrpc.php'
headers = {'Content-Type': 'application/json'}

# Replace these with your actual Zabbix username and password
username = 'Admin'
password = 'zabbix'

# Log in to the Zabbix API
login_data = {
    'jsonrpc': '2.0',
    'method': 'user.login',
    'params': {
        'user': username,
        'password': password,
    },
    'id': 1,
}
response = requests.post(url, headers=headers, json=login_data)
auth_token = response.json()['result']

# Fetch host data
host_data = {
    'jsonrpc': '2.0',
    'method': 'host.get',
    'params': {
        'output': ['hostid', 'host'],
```

```python
    'selectInterfaces': ['ip'],
    },
    'auth': auth_token,
    'id': 1,
}
response = requests.post(url, headers=headers, json=host_data)
hosts = response.json()['result']

for host in hosts:
    print(host['host'], host['interfaces'][0]['ip'])
```

The script above logs in to the Zabbix API and fetches a list of hosts along with their IP addresses. You can modify this script to fetch other types of monitoring data or to perform actions based on the data. The possibilities are virtually endless when it comes to network automation with Python and APIs. The key is to thoroughly understand the API you're working with and to have a clear idea of what tasks you want to automate.

Summary

In this chapter, we delved into the critical role of APIs in network management and the automation of network services. APIs, or Application Programming Interfaces, serve as the bridge between different software applications, enabling them to communicate and exchange data with each other. APIs are critical for network administrators as they provide the means to automate and streamline complex network operations, resulting in efficiency, accuracy, and scalability of tasks.

We began by discussing the different types of APIs used in networking, including RESTful APIs, SOAP, and GraphQL, each having its own unique advantages and use cases. Particularly, RESTful APIs are commonly preferred due to their simplicity, scalability, and stateless nature, making them ideal for internet-based applications. We then explored how Python interacts with these APIs, utilizing Python's 'requests' library to make HTTP requests to APIs, enabling the retrieval, updating, or deletion of data. We looked at various examples of how to use Python to send GET and POST requests, parse JSON responses from APIs, and handle API errors.

Lastly, we investigated the automation of network services using Python and APIs, focusing on DNS management and network monitoring. For DNS management, we learned to automate the process through a DNS provider's API, using Python to add, update, or delete DNS records automatically. In network monitoring, we explored how APIs of network monitoring tools can be used to fetch monitoring data, generate reports, or send alerts based on specific conditions. The examples provided practical insights into the extensive possibilities that APIs offer in the realm of network automation, reinforcing the importance of understanding the API's workings and having a clear goal for the tasks to automate.

CHAPTER 8: NETWORK PROGRAMMING WITH ASYNCIO

Introducing Asynchronous Programming

What is Asynchronous Programming?

Asynchronous programming is a paradigm that allows operations to execute without blocking the execution flow of your program. This is particularly useful in networking where I/O operations, such as reading and writing data to a network, are common and can potentially take a significant amount of time due to factors like network latency.

In traditional synchronous programming, the execution flow of your program is blocked while an I/O operation is performed. This means that if you send a request over the network, your program will stop and wait for the response before it continues. This can lead to inefficient use of resources, especially in scenarios where you are dealing with multiple network connections simultaneously, as is often the case in network programming.

Asynchronous programming addresses this issue by allowing the program to continue executing other tasks while waiting for the I/O operation to complete. This can lead to more efficient use of resources and improved responsiveness, especially in applications dealing with multiple simultaneous network connections.

Python supports asynchronous programming through the asyncio library, which provides an event loop, coroutines, and tasks to help you write asynchronous code. The event loop is the core of every asyncio application, and it can handle multiple I/O-bound tasks concurrently.

Why Async Programming for Networking?

The need for asynchronous programming in networking is paramount, especially when building applications like web servers, chat servers, or any service that requires handling multiple client requests simultaneously. With asynchronous programming, you can build more scalable and responsive applications.

In network automation tasks, for example, you might need to push configuration changes to hundreds or even thousands of network devices. With synchronous programming, you would have to wait for each device to respond before moving on to the next, which could be time-consuming. With asynchronous programming, you can send out all the changes simultaneously and then process the responses as they come in, leading to faster and more efficient operations.

Asynchronous programming is not just limited to networking but is also widely used in other areas such as web scraping, API integrations, and any scenario where the application has to deal with potentially slow I/O operations. However, it's worth noting that asynchronous programming can be more complex than synchronous programming due to the concurrent nature of tasks and the potential for race conditions. Care must be taken to properly synchronize tasks where necessary.

AsyncIO Library

Understanding AsyncIO

AsyncIO is a Python library that provides support for asynchronous I/O using coroutines and an event loop. It's part of the Python Standard Library, which means it comes with Python and doesn't require separate installation. However, AsyncIO is a relatively recent addition to Python and is only available in Python 3.4 and later. The library has been continuously updated and improved in subsequent Python versions, with notable enhancements in Python 3.5, 3.6, and 3.7.

AsyncIO provides several key features:

Coroutines: These are special functions that can be paused and resumed, allowing you to write asynchronous code in a synchronous style. In Python, you define a coroutine using the async def syntax. Inside a coroutine, you can use the await keyword to pause the execution until the awaited object is done.

Tasks: These are a subclass of Future that wraps coroutines. A Task is responsible for executing a coroutine object in an event loop. When a Task is created, it schedules the execution of its coroutine and can be awaited to get its result.

Event Loop: This is the core of every AsyncIO application. The event loop schedules and executes tasks and callbacks, handles I/O events, and provides mechanisms for synchronization and communication between tasks.

Futures: These are objects that represent the result of a computation that may not have completed yet. In AsyncIO, you typically don't work directly with Futures, as the library prefers using Tasks and coroutines.

Streams: AsyncIO provides high-level support for managing network I/O using streams. The library provides reader and writer objects for handling streaming I/O in a coroutine-friendly manner.

Installing AsyncIO

As mentioned earlier, AsyncIO is part of the Python Standard Library, so you don't need to install it separately. To use AsyncIO in your Python program, you just need to import it:

```python
import asyncio
```

AsyncIO presents a high-level, intuitive API for handling asynchronous programming in Python. While the inherently intricate nature of asynchronous programming introduces a learning curve, it becomes an incredibly potent tool for developing efficient and reactive network programs once you're accustomed to it.

Using AsyncIO to Run Coroutine

Let us start with a simple asyncio example. We'll create a coroutine that sleeps for a given amount of time and then prints a message.

```python
import asyncio

async def say_after(delay, what):
    await asyncio.sleep(delay)
    print(what)

asyncio.run(say_after(1, 'Hello, Asyncio!'))
```

In the above snippet, say_after is a coroutine that uses the await keyword to pause its execution for a certain delay. After the delay, it resumes execution and prints the message. The asyncio.run() function is a convenience function for running a coroutine and returning its result. It creates a new event loop, runs the given coroutine, and closes the loop.

Running Multiple Coroutines

Now let us move on to a slightly more complex example: running multiple coroutines concurrently. Below is how you can do it with asyncio:

```python
import asyncio
```

```python
async def say_after(delay, what):
    await asyncio.sleep(delay)
    print(what)

async def main():
    task1 = asyncio.create_task(say_after(1, 'Hello'))
    task2 = asyncio.create_task(say_after(2, 'Asyncio'))

    await task1
    await task2


asyncio.run(main())
```

In the above program, the main coroutine creates two tasks that run the say_after coroutine with different arguments. It then waits for both tasks to complete using the await keyword. The asyncio.create_task() function schedules a coroutine to run as a task and returns a Task object.

When you run this program, you'll see that 'Hello' is printed after 1 second and 'Asyncio' is printed after 2 seconds. However, because the tasks are running concurrently, the total runtime of the program is only 2 seconds, not 3. This is the power of asynchronous programming: it allows you to run multiple I/O-bound tasks concurrently, increasing the efficiency of your program.

Create Echo Server and Client using AsyncIO

AsyncIO provides a set of high-level APIs for building network services, including a TCP server and client. Let us take a look at how you can create a simple echo server and client using AsyncIO.

First, below is how you can create an echo server:

```python
import asyncio

async def echo_handler(reader, writer):
    data = await reader.read(100)
```

```python
    message = data.decode()
    addr = writer.get_extra_info('peername')

    print(f"Received {message} from {addr}")

    print(f"Send: {message}")
    writer.write(data)
    await writer.drain()

    print("Closing the connection")
    writer.close()

async def main():
    server = await asyncio.start_server(
        echo_handler, '127.0.0.1', 8888)

    addr = server.sockets[0].getsockname()
    print(f'Serving on {addr}')

    async with server:
        await server.serve_forever()

asyncio.run(main())
```

The echo_handler coroutine reads data from a client, sends the same data back to the client, and then closes the connection. The asyncio.start_server() function starts a TCP server that listens for connections on 127.0.0.1:8888 and uses echo_handler to handle the connections.

Next, below is how you can create an echo client that connects to the echo server and sends a message:

```python
import asyncio

async def echo_client(message):
```

```python
    reader, writer = await asyncio.open_connection('127.0.0.1', 8888)

    print(f'Send: {message}')
    writer.write(message.encode())

    data = await reader.read(100)
    print(f'Received: {data.decode()}')

    print('Closing the connection')
    writer.close()

message = 'Hello, AsyncIO!'

asyncio.run(echo_client(message))
```

The echo_client coroutine connects to the server, sends a message, receives the echoed message, and then closes the connection. The asyncio.open_connection() function opens a TCP connection to the server.

When you run the server and client programs, you should see that the client sends a message to the server, and the server echoes the message back to the client.

Concurrent Data Processing using AsyncIO

Concurrency is one of the main reasons to use asynchronous programming. Let us see how we can use asyncio for concurrent data processing.

Consider a scenario where we need to download several web pages and process the HTML data. If we did this synchronously, we would have to wait for each page to be downloaded and processed before moving on to the next one, which could be very slow if there are a lot of pages.

With asyncio, we can download and process the pages concurrently, which could significantly speed up the task. Below is how we can do this:

```python
import aiohttp
import asyncio

async def download_page(session, url):
    async with session.get(url) as response:
        return await response.text()

async def process_page(page):
    # Simulate a CPU-bound task by sleeping
    await asyncio.sleep(1)
    print(f'Page length: {len(page)}')

async def main():
    urls = ['http://example.com' for _ in range(10)]

    async with aiohttp.ClientSession() as session:
        tasks = []
        for url in urls:
            tasks.append(download_page(session, url))
        pages = await asyncio.gather(*tasks)

        tasks = []
        for page in pages:
            tasks.append(process_page(page))
        await asyncio.gather(*tasks)

# Python 3.7+
asyncio.run(main())
```

In the above program, we create a list of tasks for downloading the pages and then use asyncio.gather() to run the tasks concurrently. We then do the same for processing the pages.

The download_page() coroutine uses the aiohttp library to download a web page asynchronously. The process_page() coroutine simulates a CPU-bound task by sleeping for one second.

You can see how easy it is to run tasks concurrently with asyncio. The key is to create coroutines for the tasks and then use asyncio.gather() or asyncio.wait() to run them concurrently. Also, note that we use aiohttp.ClientSession() to create an HTTP session. This is recommended for making multiple requests because it allows aiohttp to reuse the TCP connection, which can improve performance.

Remember that asyncio is single-threaded, so it's best suited for IO-bound tasks. If you have CPU-bound tasks that could benefit from parallel execution, you might want to use a multi-threaded or multi-process approach instead.

AsyncIO for IO Bound Operations

asyncio can be used in a variety of applications to facilitate efficient IO-bound operations. Following are a few popular use cases with other Python libraries:

- Web Scraping: asyncio can be used with libraries such as aiohttp or httpx to perform concurrent web requests, significantly speeding up the process of web scraping or API data collection.

- Web Servers: asyncio is often used to build efficient, scalable web servers. Libraries such as aiohttp and fastapi can be used to build servers that can handle many concurrent connections, which is crucial for high-load web applications.

- Websockets: Libraries like websockets can leverage asyncio to build real-time applications, like chat servers, where multiple connections need to be open and managed concurrently.

- Databases: Asynchronous database libraries such as aiomysql, aiopg and aioredis allow non-blocking database operations, which can significantly improve the performance of IO-bound applications that interact heavily with databases.

- Tasks and Job Scheduling: Libraries like huey and asyncio can be combined to create asynchronous task queues and job schedulers, which can offload long running or IO-bound tasks from the main application thread and process them asynchronously.

- Networking: Libraries such as aiodns for asynchronous DNS resolutions, or aioftp for asynchronous FTP clients can be used with asyncio for efficient network programming.

- File IO: Although asyncio is mainly used for network IO, it can also be used for file IO with the aiofiles library. This can be useful for applications that need to handle many file operations concurrently.

Each of these library combinations extend the functionality of asyncio, providing specific tools for tasks such as HTTP requests, database connections, and more. Each library typically uses the same asyncio patterns (like tasks, coroutines, and futures), but provides additional functionality for their specific domain. For example, aiohttp provides an interface for making HTTP requests and responses, while aiomysql provides tools for connecting to and querying a MySQL database.

Web Scraping with aiohttp

Aiohttp is a library for making HTTP requests, and it can be used with asyncio to make these requests concurrently.

```python
import aiohttp
import asyncio


async def fetch(session, url):
    async with session.get(url) as response:
        return await response.text()


async def main():
    urls = ['http://python.org', 'http://google.com']
    async with aiohttp.ClientSession() as session:
        tasks = [fetch(session, url) for url in urls]
        htmls = await asyncio.gather(*tasks)
        for url, html in zip(urls, htmls):
            print(f'{url} page length: {len(html)}')


asyncio.run(main())
```

Below is a step-by-step breakdown of the above web scraping program:

The first two lines import the necessary libraries, aiohttp for making HTTP requests and asyncio for managing asynchronous tasks. The fetch function is an asynchronous function that takes a session and a url as arguments. This function is responsible for making a GET request to the provided URL and returning the text of the response. The async with construct is used to manage the context of the HTTP request, ensuring that resources are properly cleaned up when the request is finished.

The main function is the entry point of the program. It creates an asynchronous context for an aiohttp.ClientSession, which is a class for making HTTP requests. This session object is then passed to multiple instances of the fetch function (one for each URL), which are stored as tasks. The asyncio.gather function is used to run all the fetch tasks concurrently and wait for all of them to complete. It returns a list of results corresponding to the return values of the fetch functions.

After all the tasks have completed, the function iterates over the URLs and the corresponding HTML responses, printing the length of each response. Finally, the asyncio.run function is used to execute the main coroutine. This function creates a new event loop, runs the given coroutine, and closes the loop. The event loop is the core of every asyncio application and is responsible for executing coroutines and scheduling callbacks.

Web Server with aiohttp

You can use aiohttp to create an async web server.

```python
from aiohttp import web

async def handle(request):
    return web.Response(text="Hello, world")

app = web.Application()
app.add_routes([web.get('/', handle)])

web.run_app(app)
```

This above program creates a simple web server that responds to GET requests with "Hello, world".

handle(request): This coroutine is the request handler. It gets called whenever a GET request is received. It returns a Response object with the text "Hello, world".

web.Application(): This creates a new aiohttp web application.

app.add_routes([web.get('/', handle)]): This adds a route to the application. The route is a URL path and a coroutine function (the request handler) that gets called when a GET request is received at that path.

web.run_app(app): This starts the aiohttp web server with the application.

These examples demonstrate how asyncio can be used with other libraries to perform various tasks concurrently.

Database Access with aiomysql

Aiomysql provides an async interface for interacting with MySQL databases.

```python
import asyncio
import aiomysql

async def main():
    pool = await aiomysql.create_pool(host='127.0.0.1', port=3306,
                        user='user', password='password',
                        db='db', loop=loop)

    async with pool.acquire() as conn:
        async with conn.cursor() as cur:
            await cur.execute("SELECT 42;")
            print(await cur.fetchone())

loop = asyncio.get_event_loop()
loop.run_until_complete(main())
```

This above program queries a MySQL database for the number 42.

aiomysql.create_pool(): This coroutine creates a connection pool to a MySQL database. A connection pool is a cache of database connections that can be reused, which is more efficient than opening a new connection for each query.

pool.acquire(): This coroutine gets a connection from the pool.

conn.cursor(): This coroutine creates a new cursor object. A cursor is used to execute SQL statements.

cur.execute("SELECT 42;"): This coroutine executes an SQL statement.

cur.fetchone(): This coroutine fetches the next row of a query result set, which is the number 42 in this case.

File IO with aiofiles

Aiofiles provides an async interface for file IO.

```python
import asyncio
import aiofiles

async def write_file(data):
    async with aiofiles.open('file.txt', 'w') as f:
        await f.write(data)

async def main():
    await write_file('Hello, world!')

asyncio.run(main())
```

This above program writes "Hello, world" to a file.

aiofiles.open(): This coroutine opens a file. The 'w' argument means the file is opened for writing.

f.write(data): This coroutine writes data to the file.

In all these given programs, asyncio.run() is used to start the asyncio event loop and schedule a coroutine to run. This is the main entry point for asyncio programs, and it takes care of creating and cleaning up the event loop, so you don't have to do it manually.

Summary

This chapter provided an in-depth exploration of asynchronous programming in Python, focusing on the asyncio library. Asynchronous programming, as opposed to synchronous or sequential programming, allows for the execution of certain tasks simultaneously. This is critical in networking where tasks such as sending or receiving data packets, interacting with APIs, or querying databases may block execution, thus slowing down the entire process. Utilizing asyncio, we learned to develop concurrent tasks, allowing multiple operations to progress concurrently, significantly improving the efficiency of network programs.

We delved into the asyncio library, examining its features and practical applications. We learned to create and manage asyncio event loops, crucial for scheduling and executing coroutines. Using aiohttp, we performed concurrent web scraping. We also created a simple web server that could handle multiple requests concurrently. We then interfaced asyncio with aiomysql to perform concurrent database operations, demonstrating how asyncio can be used to prevent blocking during database access. Lastly, we explored aiofiles for asynchronous file operations, providing a way to handle file I/O that doesn't block the event loop.

The chapter wrapped up by demonstrating the compatibility of asyncio with other Python libraries, highlighting the versatility of asynchronous programming. We showed how aiohttp can be used for concurrent web requests, aiomysql for non-blocking database access, and aiofiles for non-blocking file I/O. Each of these libraries leverages asyncio's capabilities, extending the benefits of asynchronous programming to various domains. By integrating these libraries, we can build complex, efficient, and responsive network applications with Python.

CHAPTER 9: NETWORK TESTING AND SIMULATION

Introduction to Network Testing and Simulation

Network testing and simulation are pivotal aspects of maintaining and improving network performance. They provide valuable insights into how the network behaves under different conditions, which can help identify potential issues, bottlenecks, and vulnerabilities. Ultimately, this leads to more reliable, secure, and efficient networks.

Network testing methodologies focus on assessing various aspects of the network, including performance, reliability, capacity, and security. Performance testing measures metrics like throughput, latency, packet loss, and jitter to evaluate how well the network can handle data transfer. Reliability testing checks network stability and resilience in different situations, including hardware failures, software crashes, and high traffic load. Capacity testing evaluates the maximum amount of data the network can handle without performance degradation. Security testing aims at identifying vulnerabilities that could be exploited by attackers, helping to enhance network security.

Python offers several libraries for network testing and simulation. Some notable ones include Scapy, Locust, and NetworkX. Scapy allows for packet crafting and network scanning, offering a flexible tool for network discovery and security testing. Locust is a load testing tool, which can simulate thousands of users to assess network performance under heavy traffic. NetworkX is a powerful library for the creation, manipulation, and study of complex networks, offering a wide range of algorithms for network analysis.

Network simulations are essential for predicting network behavior under different scenarios without the risk and cost of testing on the actual network. It involves creating a model of the network and running simulations to observe its behavior. Python's SimPy library is widely used for creating network simulations. It allows you to define custom network models and run simulations to analyze network behavior and performance.

Overall, network testing and simulation are crucial in the network life cycle. They offer a proactive approach to discovering and resolving network issues, contributing significantly to network optimization, and ensuring the network can meet its performance requirements. Regular testing and simulation should be an integral part of any network management strategy to ensure optimal network performance and reliability.

Popular Network Testing Methodologies

In the realm of network operations, various testing methodologies exist to ascertain the performance, reliability, capacity, and security of the network. These methodologies are critical in ensuring the network operates at its optimal level, providing a secure and reliable medium for data transfer. Furthermore, Python, renowned for its extensive libraries and straightforward syntax, presents itself as an invaluable tool in executing these tests.

Let us break down these network testing methodologies and look at how they can be practically applied.

Performance Testing

Performance Testing is a critical methodology that evaluates the network's speed, scalability, and stability under different workloads. It focuses on key metrics such as throughput, latency, packet loss, and jitter. Throughput refers to the amount of data successfully transferred over a specific period. Latency measures the delay in data transfer, packet loss accounts for the data that never reaches its destination, and jitter is the variation in delay of received packets.

Python's ping3 library is an excellent tool for measuring latency and packet loss. It provides a simple interface for sending ICMP Echo Request (ping) packets and processing the responses. On the other hand, iperf3, accessible through the iperf3-python library, is commonly used for measuring throughput. It creates a data stream between two computers and measures the speed at which data travels from one to the other, providing an accurate measurement of the network's bandwidth.

Reliability Testing

Reliability Testing is another vital methodology that checks the network's ability to operate without failure over a specific period. This type of testing often involves stress testing, which intentionally subjects the network to high loads or challenging conditions to observe its reaction. The locust library in Python can simulate high-load scenarios, enabling you to define user behavior in your Python code and test how your network manages multiple users or connections simultaneously.

Capacity Testing

Capacity Testing is a methodology that helps determine the maximum load a network can handle without compromising performance. This is crucial for planning network growth and averting performance issues as the network demand increases. Tools like iperf3-python can measure the maximum throughput the network can handle, providing an accurate understanding of its capacity. Alternatively, the locust library can be used to emulate many simultaneous connections and observe how the network performs under such conditions.

<u>Security Testing</u>

Security Testing is a comprehensive methodology that identifies potential vulnerabilities in the network that could be exploited by attackers. This includes penetration testing, where you proactively attack your own network to discover vulnerabilities, and vulnerability scanning, where the network is automatically scanned for known vulnerabilities.

Python's scapy library is a potent tool for security testing. With scapy, you can construct custom packets, analyze network traffic, and even perform rudimentary penetration testing tasks. For vulnerability scanning, a tool like OpenVAS can be used. Although OpenVAS isn't a Python library, it does provide a Python API, allowing you to use Python scripts to automate and customize your scans.

In essence, each of these testing methodologies plays a vital role in ensuring optimal and secure network performance. They offer the ability to proactively identify and rectify issues, thereby preventing potentially catastrophic network failures. Python, with its wide array of libraries and straightforward syntax, is an exceptional tool for implementing these network testing methodologies. By leveraging Python's capabilities, network operators can ensure the seamless operation of their networks, thereby guaranteeing reliable and secure data transfer.

Performance Testing using ping3 and iperf3

<u>ping3</u>

The ping3 library is a valuable tool in Python's vast ecosystem, providing a pure python3 implementation of the ICMP ping command. This utility allows users to check network connectivity by sending echo request packets to a specific host and waiting for an echo response. It serves as a straightforward mechanism to verify if a remote host is active or reachable over the network. Additionally, it measures the round-trip time for these packets, thereby giving a reliable estimate of the latency or delay between your system and the remote host.

To install ping3, you can use pip:

```
pip install ping3
```

Below is an example of how to use ping3:

```python
from ping3 import ping, verbose_ping

print(ping('google.com'))  # Returns delay in seconds.
verbose_ping('google.com')  # Prints the result in console.
```

In the above code snippet, we're using ping to measure the latency to google.com. The ping function returns the delay in seconds, while verbose_ping prints a more detailed result.

iperf3-python

The iperf3-python library is essentially a Python wrapper for iperf3, a highly versatile tool used widely in the field of network engineering for conducting active measurements of the maximum achievable bandwidth on Internet Protocol (IP) networks. The fundamental function of iperf3 is to create a data stream between two nodes in an IP network and measure the speed of data transfer between them. By wrapping this functionality in Python, iperf3-python provides network engineers with an accessible and flexible interface for conducting these measurements. This allows them to integrate network testing into broader Python scripts, thereby automating testing procedures and facilitating more complex network analyses.

To install iperf3-python, you can use pip:

```
pip install iperf3
```

Below is an example of how to use iperf3-python:

```python
import iperf3

client = iperf3.Client()
client.duration = 1
client.server_hostname = 'iperf.scottlinux.com'
client.port = 5201

result = client.run()

if result.error:
```

```python
    print(f"Error: {result.error}")
else:
    print(f"Average Sent Speed: {result.sent_Mbps} Mbps")
    print(f"Average Received Speed: {result.received_Mbps} Mbps")
```

In the above code snippet, we're creating an iperf3 client and setting it to run for 1 second. We're specifying the server hostname and port (you can change this to your server's details). The run function runs the test and returns a result object that contains the results of the test, including the average sent and received speeds.

Remember, the server you are testing against must be running an iperf3 server. You can set one up yourself on a separate machine, or you can use a public iperf3 server, like the one in the example.

Reliability Testing using Locust

Reliability testing is a crucial aspect of network testing that assesses the capability of a system or component to consistently perform its required functions under specified conditions over a given duration. This methodology is essential as it provides valuable insights into the robustness of the network system and its dependability, especially in instances where uninterrupted service is critical. In the landscape of network services, the application of reliability testing often entails bombarding a server or service with high volumes of traffic and meticulously tracking its response over a particular period. This approach helps in unearthing potential issues that might go unnoticed under regular load conditions, but reveal themselves when the network is under significant stress. Such issues could range from minor performance degradations to critical failures, all of which could have substantial impacts on the overall network performance and user experience.

Locust, an open-source load testing tool, is highly recommended for reliability testing in Python. This tool is not only powerful but also versatile, allowing developers to define user behavior using Python code. By modeling different types of user behavior, developers can create realistic load scenarios that closely mimic the demands a system may face in a production environment.

Once these user behaviors are defined, Locust enables your system to be swarmed with millions of these simulated users concurrently. This swarming process subjects your network to an immense load, thereby providing a stringent test of its endurance and reliability. The results from these tests offer valuable data on how well the system can handle high traffic, identify bottlenecks, and ultimately determine if the system can reliably handle real-world usage scenarios.

To install Locust, you can use pip:

```
pip install locust
```

Below is a simple program of how to use Locust:

```python
from locust import HttpUser, task, between

class WebsiteUser(HttpUser):
    wait_time = between(5, 15)

    @task
    def index(self):
        self.client.get("/")
```

In the above code snippet, we're defining a single user type, WebsiteUser, that waits between 5 and 15 seconds (chosen randomly) between tasks, and has a single task: sending a GET request to the homepage.

To run this test, save it to a file, say locustfile.py, then run locust -f locustfile.py in the command line. This will start a Locust instance. You can then go to http://localhost:8089 in your browser to start a swarm of users.

After running the Locust test, you'll be presented with an interactive web-based interface at http://localhost:8089 that provides real-time statistics about the test that's being run. This interface provides various statistics like the number of requests per second, the number of users, the average response time, the min/max response times, and the number of failed requests.

Once you start a test (or a "swarm"), you input the number of total users to simulate and the spawn rate (users to start per second). When the test is running, Locust will display a constantly updating table of statistics, for example:

Name	# reqs	# fails	Avg	Min	Max	Median	req/s	failures/s
GET /	131	0(0.00%)	50	34	101	47	0.50	0.00
Aggregated	131	0(0.00%)	50	34	101	47	0.50	0.00

In the given output, the table shows that 131 GET requests have been made to the root ("/") of the website, none of these requests have failed, the average response time is 50ms, the minimum response time is 34ms, the maximum response time is 101ms, and the median response time is 47ms. The last two columns show the number of requests and failures per second.

The web interface also provides charts to visualize the number of requests per second, users load, response times, and other metrics over time. Remember that the purpose of these tests is to measure the reliability and robustness of your network services. If you see a high number of failures, or if the response times are longer than expected, it could indicate a problem that needs to be addressed.

Capacity Testing using Locust

Capacity testing is a crucial aspect of performance testing designed to ascertain the maximum load a system can accommodate without performance degradation. The process involves methodically escalating the load on the system until it attains its operational limit. The point of failure or performance dip provides insights into the system's capacity, enabling informed decisions about scaling, resource allocation, and infrastructure improvement.

To perform capacity testing, tools like Locust can be employed effectively. Earlier, we discussed using Locust for reliability testing, where it was used to simulate specific load conditions. However, in capacity testing, its application differs slightly. In this case, you incrementally ramp up the load using Locust to uncover the system's breaking point. This enables you to identify potential bottlenecks and thresholds, providing a clear understanding of how much traffic the system can handle before it starts to falter.

Below is an example using the same HTTP server we used before:

```python
from locust import HttpUser, task, between

class WebsiteUser(HttpUser):
    wait_time = between(1, 2.5)

    @task
    def load_page(self):
        self.client.get("/")
```

In this script, WebsiteUser is simulating a user of your HTTP service. The load_page function is decorated with the @task decorator, which means that it's a task that a WebsiteUser will perform. In this case, load_page is simply loading the root ("/") of your website.

wait_time is a property of HttpUser that defines how long a simulated user should wait between executing tasks. In this case, each user will wait between 1 and 2.5 seconds.

You can run this script with locust -f your_script.py and then access the Locust web interface at http://localhost:8089. From there, you can start a "swarm" and gradually increase the number of users until you notice the system's performance starting to degrade. This will give you an idea of the capacity of your system.

Network Simulation using Simpy

Network simulation is a technique where a program models the behavior of a network by calculating the interaction between the different network entities (routers, switches, nodes, access points, links etc.) using mathematical formulas. Network simulation software allows you to make a detailed study and analysis of the performance of networks without having the actual hardware.

Python provides several libraries for network simulation, one of the most popular is SimPy.

SimPy is a process-based discrete-event simulation framework based on standard Python and is a very good choice for building complex network simulations.

SimPy

SimPy allows you to create so-called "processes", which are Python generator functions that can be paused and resumed. These processes live in an environment and interact with it and with each other via events.

SimPy is used in networking to simulate packet transmission, queue management, congestion control, and other network behaviors.

Installing SimPy

You can install SimPy using pip:

```
pip install simpy
```

Usage of SimPy

Below is a simple example of a SimPy simulation. This is not a network simulation yet, but it demonstrates the basic concept of processes and events in SimPy:

```python
import simpy

def car(env):
    while True:
        print('Start parking at %d' % env.now)
        parking_duration = 5
        yield env.timeout(parking_duration)

        print('Start driving at %d' % env.now)
        trip_duration = 2
        yield env.timeout(trip_duration)

env = simpy.Environment()
env.process(car(env))
env.run(until=15)
```

In the above program, the car function is a process that alternates between parking and driving. The env.timeout() function call creates an event that will trigger after a certain amount of simulated time has passed.

Now, let us translate this concept to a network simulation. A basic network simulation might involve simulating packet transmissions over a network link with a certain bandwidth. In SimPy, you could model the link as a resource with a limited capacity, and packets as processes that request a certain amount of that resource for a certain amount of time.

Below is a simple example of how you might do this:

```python
import simpy

class Packet(object):
    def __init__(self, env, id, link, size):
        self.env = env
        self.id = id
        self.size = size
        self.link = link

    def send(self):
        print('Packet {} sending at {}'.format(self.id, self.env.now))
        transmission_time = self.size / self.link.bandwidth
        yield self.env.timeout(transmission_time)
        print('Packet {} sent at {}'.format(self.id, self.env.now))

class Link(object):
    def __init__(self, env, bandwidth):
        self.env = env
        self.bandwidth = bandwidth

env = simpy.Environment()
link = Link(env, 1000)  # Bandwidth in bits per second


# Create 5 packets and schedule them to be sent at different times
```

```python
for i in range(5):
    packet = Packet(env, i, link, 2000)  # Size in bits
    env.process(packet.send())
    env.run(until=5)
```

In the above program, Packet is a class representing network packets. Each packet has a size and is sent over a Link with a certain bandwidth. The send method calculates the time it takes to transmit the packet based on its size and the link's bandwidth, then yields a timeout event for that duration.

Let us look at a slightly more complex example. In this scenario, we establish a network comprising two nodes linked together. Each node dispatches packets to the other via this link, which has a fixed bandwidth. When the link is fully engaged, a buffer comes into play, storing the incoming packets temporarily. This setup allows us to observe network behaviors such as packet queuing, latency, and potential packet loss, crucial for understanding the network's performance under varying conditions.

```python
import simpy

class Packet(object):
    def __init__(self, time, size, destination):
        self.time = time
        self.size = size
        self.destination = destination

class Node(object):
    def __init__(self, env, id, link, rate):
        self.env = env
        self.id = id
        self.link = link
        self.rate = rate
        self.action = env.process(self.run())

    def run(self):
        while True:
```

```python
            yield self.env.timeout(1 / self.rate)
            packet = Packet(self.env.now, 1000, 1 - self.id)
            print(f"Node {self.id} sends packet at {self.env.now}")
            self.env.process(self.link.transmit(packet))


class Link(object):
    def __init__(self, env, bandwidth):
        self.env = env
        self.bandwidth = bandwidth
        self.queue = simpy.Store(env)


    def transmit(self, packet):
        yield self.queue.put(packet)
        while packet:
            with self.queue.get() as got_packet:
                yield got_packet
                transmission_time = packet.size / self.bandwidth
                yield self.env.timeout(transmission_time)
                print(f"Packet from Node {packet.destination} received at
{self.env.now}")
                packet = None


env = simpy.Environment()
link = Link(env, 1000)
nodes = [Node(env, i, link, 2) for i in range(2)]
env.run(until=10)
```

This script simulates two nodes (Node 0 and Node 1) sending packets to each other over
a single link. Each node sends a packet to the other node at a rate of 2 packets per second.
The link has a bandwidth of 1000 bits per second and a buffer that can store an unlimited
number of packets. When the link is busy transmitting a packet, incoming packets are
stored in the buffer until the link is free.

When you run this script, you should see output indicating when each node sends a packet and when each packet is received.

The above program demonstrates a very simple network, but you can extend it to simulate more complex networks. For instance, you could add more nodes and links to create a network topology, simulate different types of traffic (e.g., TCP and UDP), or implement congestion control algorithms.

Network Performance

Network performance can be improved by implementing various strategies and best practices. However, the exact methods will depend on the specific network conditions and requirements. Following are some general steps you can take:

Understanding the Network State

The first step in improving network performance is understanding your network's current state. This includes knowing the network topology, bandwidth usage, traffic patterns, and any existing issues or bottlenecks. Network monitoring and testing tools can provide this information. For example, the Python libraries we've discussed earlier, such as ping3, iperf3, locust, and simpy, can be used to measure network performance and simulate different network conditions.

Identifying Issues

Once you have a clear understanding of your network, you can start to identify any issues or bottlenecks that may be affecting performance. This could include high network latency, packet loss, bandwidth limitations, or inefficient routing. Network testing and simulation tools can help identify these issues.

Implementing Improvements

After identifying the issues, you can start implementing improvements. This could involve a wide range of actions depending on the identified issues.

Following are some potential improvements:

- Optimize Network Configuration: Incorrect network configurations can lead to poor performance. Check your network devices and make sure they're configured correctly.

- Upgrade Network Infrastructure: If the network devices are outdated or if the network is regularly hitting its bandwidth capacity, it might be time to upgrade the network infrastructure.

- Load Balancing: If certain network paths or servers are being overused while others are underused, implementing load balancing can help distribute network traffic more evenly.

- Quality of Service (QoS): QoS settings can prioritize certain types of traffic to ensure that important data gets through even when the network is busy.

- Implement Caching: Caching can significantly reduce bandwidth usage and improve response times by storing a copy of frequently accessed data closer to the users.

Ongoing Monitoring and Testing

Network performance should be continuously monitored and periodically tested to identify any new issues that arise and to ensure that the implemented improvements are having the desired effect. Regularly updating and patching network devices can also help to maintain network performance and security.

Remember, improving network performance often involves a combination of different strategies and requires continuous effort. It's not a one-time task, but an ongoing process.

Summary

In this chapter, we delved into network testing and network simulations, crucial aspects of network performance enhancement. The chapter began with an overview of various network testing methodologies, including performance, reliability, and capacity testing. Each of these methodologies offers a unique perspective on the network's functioning, identifying potential bottlenecks and issues that could affect the network's performance.

Performance testing, involving ping3 and iperf3, provides insights into latency, bandwidth, and the overall speed of the network. Reliability testing, with the use of locust, helps measure a system's stability over time and under stress. Capacity testing gives an understanding of the maximum load the network can handle. All these testing methods offer a comprehensive view of the network's health and are instrumental in identifying areas of improvement.

The latter part of the chapter introduced the concept of network simulations, specifically using simpy, enabling us to model and predict network behavior under various conditions.

Through simulations, it's possible to preemptively identify potential issues and optimize the network for better performance. Lastly, we discussed how continuous monitoring, testing, and the implementation of various improvement strategies can significantly enhance network performance. These strategies include optimizing network configuration, upgrading network infrastructure, implementing load balancing and caching, and setting Quality of Service (QoS) priorities.

CHAPTER 10: NETWORK CONFIGURATION MANAGEMENT

Network Configuration Management

About Network Configuration

Network configuration refers to the setup of a network's components, including routers, switches, firewalls, load balancers, servers, and other network devices. It details how these components are interconnected, the protocols they use to communicate, their IP address assignments, and their security settings. The configuration of a network is crucial to its performance, security, and reliability, and it often needs to be fine-tuned to meet the specific requirements of a business or application.

There are several types of network configurations, which depend on the network's size, purpose, and the physical and logical arrangement of its devices. For instance, in a star configuration, all devices connect to a central hub. In a bus configuration, all devices share a common communication line. In a ring configuration, each device connects to exactly two other devices, forming a loop. And in a mesh configuration, devices are interconnected, with multiple paths between any two nodes.

Network configurations can also be categorized based on the protocols they use. For instance, TCP/IP networks, the most common type of network today, are configured with IP addresses, subnet masks, gateways, and DNS servers. Other network types include IPX/SPX networks (used primarily in systems that implement the Novell NetWare protocol suite) and AppleTalk networks (used in older Apple devices).

Network Configuration Management is the process of organizing and maintaining information about all the components of a network. It involves the collection and management of configuration data to ensure network resources are correctly configured and that the network is operating at optimal performance and reliability. It is a critical aspect of network administration, involving the tracking of individual devices, software, and other network components, ensuring they are properly set up, and monitoring their status over time.

Benefit of Network Configuration Management

The benefits of Network Configuration Management include improved network security (by ensuring that security settings are correctly configured and updated), reduced downtime (by quickly identifying and correcting configuration errors that can cause network failures), and improved operational efficiency (by automating routine configuration tasks, freeing up network administrators to focus on other tasks). Network Configuration Management also provides a record of changes made to the network configuration, which can be crucial for troubleshooting problems and for compliance with regulatory requirements.

Network Configuration Management can be a complex task, especially for large networks with many devices. Fortunately, several Python libraries, such as NAPALM and Netmiko, can help automate many aspects of network configuration and management. These tools provide an interface for sending configuration commands to network devices, retrieving their current configuration, and comparing configurations over time. This can significantly simplify the task of Network Configuration Management, making the network more reliable and easier to maintain.

NAPALM Library

What is NAPALM?

NAPALM (Network Automation and Programmability Abstraction Layer with Multivendor support) is a Python library that provides a unified API to different networking devices. It was designed to simplify and abstract some of the complexities of working with different network device interfaces. The name NAPALM signifies its purpose: a tool that allows network engineers to drop 'fire' onto their networks and watch them melt into a consistent, programmable interface.

The primary features of NAPALM include:

- Multi-vendor support: NAPALM supports a wide range of networking devices from different vendors, including Arista, Cisco, Juniper, and others.

- Consistent API: Regardless of the underlying device type or operating system, the API remains consistent.

- Configurations management: With NAPALM, you can retrieve the current configuration, replace or merge it, and rollback configurations if needed.

- Operational state data: NAPALM allows you to fetch operational state data such as ARP tables, BGP neighbors, MAC tables, and others.

Installing NAPALM

To install NAPALM, you can use pip:

```
pip install napalm
```

Once NAPALM is installed, you can start using it to interact with your network devices.

Below is a simple program of how you might use NAPALM to connect to a device and retrieve some information:

```python
import napalm

# Create a driver for the device type (e.g., 'ios', 'junos', 'eos', etc.)
driver = napalm.get_network_driver('ios')

# Create a connection to the device
device = driver(hostname='10.0.0.1', username='admin', password='password')

# Open the connection
device.open()

# Get facts about the device
facts = device.get_facts()

# Print the facts
for key, value in facts.items():
    print(f"{key}: {value}")

# Close the connection
device.close()
```

In the above program, get_facts() retrieves some basic information about the device, such as the model, serial number, uptime, etc. NAPALM provides many other methods for interacting with the device, such as get_interfaces(), get_bgp_neighbors(), and get_config(). Please note that you should replace 'ios', '10.0.0.1', 'admin', and 'password' with the actual driver type, device IP, username, and password of the network device you're trying to connect to. And, always remember to close the connection when you're done. This releases resources on both your machine and the network device.

Version Control and Network Configuration Backup

Version control and backup of network configurations are essential for managing network infrastructures. By using version control systems such as Git, we can track changes over time, identify who made a change, and roll back changes if an issue arises.

NAPALM, as mentioned before, is a Python library that simplifies the process of interacting with network devices. While it doesn't directly integrate with version control systems, we can combine it with tools such as Git to manage network configurations effectively.

The following steps provide an example of how you might use NAPALM to retrieve network configurations and store them in a Git repository.

Install Necessary Libraries

Install the NAPALM and GitPython libraries, which provide the functionality we need to interact with network devices and Git repositories, respectively.

```
pip install napalm gitpython
```

Retrieve the Network Configuration

We use NAPALM to connect to the network device and retrieve the current configuration.

```python
import napalm

def get_config(hostname, username, password, driver_name):
    driver = napalm.get_network_driver(driver_name)
    with driver(hostname, username, password) as device:
        return device.get_config()

config = get_config('10.0.0.1', 'admin', 'password', 'ios')
```

In this code, we define a function get_config that uses NAPALM to retrieve the configuration of a network device. The with statement ensures that the connection to the device is closed after we retrieve the configuration.

Store Configuration in Git

Next, we use GitPython to store the retrieved configuration in a Git repository.

```python
from git import Repo

def save_config_to_git(config, repo_path, commit_message):
    repo = Repo(repo_path)
    with open(f"{repo_path}/config.txt", 'w') as f:
        f.write(config)
    repo.git.add('--all')
    repo.git.commit('-m', commit_message)


save_config_to_git(config, '/path/to/your/repo', 'Add initial config')
```

This function save_config_to_git takes the configuration, a path to a Git repository, and a commit message. It writes the configuration to a file in the repository, then adds the file to the staging area and commits it.

After performing all the above steps, you now have a version-controlled backup of your network configuration. If the configuration of the network device changes, you can retrieve the new configuration and commit it to the Git repository. You can also push your changes to a remote repository to have an off-site backup.

And, do not forget to replace '10.0.0.1', 'admin', 'password', 'ios', and '/path/to/your/repo' with your actual device IP, username, password, driver type, and path to your Git repository.

Automating Network Configuration

Automating network configuration changes can be a significant advantage in maintaining a network as it reduces human error and increases efficiency. We will continue to use the NAPALM library for this.

Before proceeding, keep in mind that any changes to network configurations should be done carefully, as incorrect settings can lead to network disruptions.

Let us see how we can automate network configuration changes using NAPALM:

Load the New Configuration

Let us assume you have a configuration file called new_config.txt with the configuration changes you want to apply. You can load this configuration into the network device using the load_merge_candidate method, which merges the current configuration with the new one.

```python
import napalm


def load_config(hostname, username, password, driver_name, config_file):
    driver = napalm.get_network_driver(driver_name)
    with driver(hostname, username, password) as device:
        device.load_merge_candidate(filename=config_file)


load_config('10.0.0.1', 'admin', 'password', 'ios', 'new_config.txt')
```

This function opens a connection to the network device, loads the new configuration, and merges it with the existing one.

Commit the Changes

After loading the new configuration, you need to commit the changes for them to take effect. If you're satisfied with the changes, you can commit them using the commit_config method.

```python
def commit_config(hostname, username, password, driver_name):
    driver = napalm.get_network_driver(driver_name)
    with driver(hostname, username, password) as device:
        device.commit_config()


commit_config('10.0.0.1', 'admin', 'password', 'ios')
```

This function commits any pending configuration changes on the network device.

<u>Verify the Changes</u>

After committing the changes, you should verify that they have been applied correctly. You can do this by retrieving the current configuration and checking that it contains the expected settings.

```python
def verify_config(hostname, username, password, driver_name):
    driver = napalm.get_network_driver(driver_name)
    with driver(hostname, username, password) as device:
        return device.get_config()


print(verify_config('10.0.0.1', 'admin', 'password', 'ios'))
```

This function retrieves and prints the current configuration of the network device.

Again, do not forget to replace '10.0.0.1', 'admin', 'password', 'ios', and 'new_config.txt' with your actual device IP, username, password, driver type, and path to your configuration file.

Summary

In this chapter, we delved into Network Configuration Management and its importance in maintaining robust and efficient networks. We learned that network configurations are the detailed settings related to the operational parameters of network devices. These configurations, if not managed correctly, can lead to system vulnerabilities, inconsistencies, and network failures. We also explored the different types of network configurations, such as initial configurations, functional configurations, and performance configurations. Network Configuration Management, a crucial aspect of network management, ensures the network's optimal performance by maintaining, updating, and backing up these configurations.

We then explored the NAPALM (Network Automation and Programmability Abstraction Layer with Multivendor support) library, a Python library that standardizes how we interact with different network devices. We learned how to install and use NAPALM to connect to network devices, retrieve their configurations, and even change the configurations. NAPALM's ability to support multiple vendors and platforms makes it a versatile tool for network configuration management.

Finally, we examined how to automate network configuration changes using NAPALM, which can significantly reduce manual errors and increase efficiency. We learned to load new configurations onto a network device, commit these changes, and verify the changes. This automation process allows network administrators to manage complex network configurations more efficiently. We also discussed the importance of version control and backup in preserving network configurations, ensuring the network's stability and minimizing potential disruptions due to misconfigurations.

Chapter 11: Ansible and Python

Introduction to Ansible

Ansible is an open-source automation tool that provides a powerful, flexible framework for managing and configuring systems. It uses a declarative language to describe system configuration, allowing administrators to define what they want the system to look like, rather than specifying the steps to get there. This makes it easier to manage complex systems and reduces the likelihood of errors due to manual configuration changes.

In the context of network automation, Ansible allows you to manage the configurations of network devices, automate repetitive tasks, and coordinate complex sets of actions across multiple devices. By defining your network configuration in Ansible, you can ensure consistency across all devices, reduce the time needed for configuration updates, and minimize the potential for manual errors. Ansible uses a simple, human-readable data serialization language called YAML to define automation jobs, which it calls 'playbooks'. These playbooks can be used to automate tasks such as software installations, service configurations, and updates. Ansible works by connecting to your nodes (the systems you're managing) and pushing out small programs, called 'Ansible modules', to them. These programs are written in Python, which makes Ansible especially relevant in the context of network automation with Python. Once these programs are executed on the nodes, they communicate back with the Ansible machine, remove themselves from the nodes, and provide information back to Ansible about what happened.

Python is the backend of Ansible, meaning that Ansible's modules, which are used to interact with system resources like services, packages, or files, are written in Python. This means that, if you're already working with Python for network automation, learning Ansible can leverage your existing skills and knowledge. Another significant advantage of Ansible is that it's agentless. Unlike other configuration management tools, it doesn't require you to install any software on the nodes it manages. It communicates over standard SSH (or WinRM for Windows nodes), which makes it easy to set up and reduces the potential for conflicts with other software. Ansible is also highly flexible and can be used in combination with other tools for more complex automation tasks. For instance, you can use Ansible to orchestrate more complex automation workflows, integrate with CI/CD pipelines, or manage multi-tier applications.

Setting up Ansible on Windows

Installing Ansible on Windows is a little tricky because Ansible does not run directly on Windows. However, you can run Ansible within a Windows Subsystem for Linux (WSL) environment, or you can run Ansible in a Docker container, or in a virtual machine running Linux. Following are the steps to install Ansible on Windows using WSL:

Install Windows Subsystem for Linux (WSL)

Open PowerShell as Administrator and run:

```
wsl --install
```

This command will install WSL with the default Linux distribution (Ubuntu). If you want to use another distribution, you can select it from the Microsoft Store after installing WSL.

Update and Upgrade WSL:

Launch your WSL Linux distribution (e.g., Ubuntu) from the Start menu.

Update your package lists:

```
sudo apt-get update
```

Upgrade your installed packages:

```
sudo apt-get upgrade
```

Install Ansible

Still within WSL, install the software-properties-common package (this provides the add-apt-repository command):

```
sudo apt-get install software-properties-common
```

Add the Ansible PPA:

```
sudo apt-add-repository --yes --update ppa:ansible/ansible
```

```
sudo apt-get install ansible
```

Verify Installation:
You can verify the installation by running:

```
ansible --version
```

This should print the installed Ansible version.

It's a good practice to create a virtual environment for your Python projects. You can install the venv module if it's not already installed:

```
sudo apt-get install python3-venv
```

Navigate to your project directory and create a new virtual environment:

```
python3 -m venv env
```

Activate the virtual environment:

```
source env/bin/activate
```

Now, you can install any Python packages you need for your project using pip, and they will be installed into the virtual environment. The above steps should guide you to have a working Ansible installation within a Python virtual environment on Windows. You can use Ansible to define and run your network automation tasks, and use Python to write custom Ansible modules if needed.

Ansible Modules, Tasks and Playbooks

In Ansible, modules, tasks, and playbooks are the key components to define and orchestrate automation.

Modules

In the context of Ansible, a module is a standalone script that can be used by the Ansible API or by the ansible or ansible-playbook CLI command. Modules are like the tools in Ansible's toolbox. They perform specific functions and are designed to be idempotent, which means they can be run multiple times without causing redundant changes.

For example, there's a module called ping that just checks if you can connect to your targets. There's a command module that can execute arbitrary commands. There are also a lot of specialized modules for different systems, like apt or yum for package management, file for managing files, copy for copying files, and many more.

Tasks

A task is nothing but a call to an Ansible module. It represents a single step in your automation process. You can think of a task as an application of a module. Tasks are defined within a playbook and have a name and a module. They may also have some additional parameters depending on the module. For example, if you're using the command module, the command you want to run would be one of the parameters.

Playbooks

Playbooks are at the heart of Ansible's operation, and they're where tasks are defined. They are written in YAML format and describe the desired state of something, not the steps to get there. A playbook contains one or more "plays". Each play is a mapping between a set of hosts (known as the inventory) and a set of tasks. When a playbook is run, Ansible executes each play in order, and for each play, it runs each task in order on every host the play applies to.

In a playbook, you might have a play that targets your web servers and another play that targets your database servers. Within each play, you would have tasks that use modules to install necessary packages, configure settings, start services, etc.

An example of a simple playbook might look like this:

```
- name: install and start apache
  hosts: webservers
  tasks:
  - name: install apache
    yum:
      name: httpd
      state: present
  - name: start apache
    service:
      name: httpd
```

    state: started

In this playbook, there's a single play that targets hosts in the webservers group. The play has two tasks: one uses the yum module to install the httpd package, and the other uses the service module to start the httpd service.

Inventory

Another important concept in Ansible is the inventory. This is a list of nodes that Ansible will manage. Nodes are typically servers, but they can also be things like network devices, or even cloud resources. The inventory is defined in a file (by default, this file is called hosts and is located in /etc/ansible).

You can specify nodes using their hostname or IP address, and you can also group nodes together. For example:

```
[webservers]
web1.example.com
web2.example.com


[dbservers]
db1.example.com
```

In this inventory file, there are two groups of nodes: webservers and dbservers. You can target groups in your playbooks.

Variables and Facts

Ansible allows you to use variables to deal with differences between systems. For example, you might have a variable for the version of a package you want to install, or for the name of a service you want to start. Ansible also gathers information about the nodes it manages in variables called facts. Facts are things like the node's IP addresses, its operating system, and so on. You can use facts in your playbooks to make decisions or change the behavior of tasks.

Roles

Roles in Ansible provide a framework for fully independent, or interdependent collections of variables, tasks, files, templates, and modules. In other words, roles are a way to group related tasks together and make them reusable. This allows you to share your automation and collaborate with others.

For example, you might have a role for setting up a web server. This role would include tasks for installing the necessary packages, writing the configuration file, and starting the service.

To tie it all together, below is what a simple Ansible setup might look like:

- An inventory file that lists all your nodes and groups them into webservers and dbservers.

- A playbook that uses the yum and service modules to install and start Apache. The playbook targets the webservers group in the inventory.

- A variable for the name of the package to install (httpd).

- To run this playbook, you would use the ansible-playbook command:

```
ansible-playbook -i inventory playbook.yml
```

- This command tells Ansible to use the specified inventory file and run the specified playbook.

Ansible connects to each node in turn, gathers facts, and then runs each task on each node. If a task is already in its desired state (for example, if the httpd package is already installed), Ansible skips it.

My First Ansible Script

To get started with Ansible, we need to create our first playbook. As mentioned, a playbook is a YAML file containing a series of tasks to be performed on managed nodes. For simplicity's sake, let us start by creating a playbook that installs the latest version of the Apache web server on our managed nodes.

Define Your Inventory

First, we need to define our inventory. In the simplest form, an inventory is a text file with a list of hostnames, one per line. Below is an example:

```
# inventory.txt
192.168.1.10
192.168.1.11
```

This inventory file represents two nodes with the IP addresses 192.168.1.10 and 192.168.1.11.

Create the Playbook

Next, we create a playbook. Let us name it apache.yml. In this playbook, we define a single play that targets all nodes (hosts: all) and installs Apache (httpd package in most Linux distributions).

```
# apache.yml
---
- hosts: all
  become: yes
  tasks:
    - name: Ensure Apache is installed
      package:
        name: httpd
        state: present
```

The become: yes line tells Ansible to execute the tasks with superuser privileges, as installing a package typically requires these.

Run the Playbook

We're now ready to run our playbook. Below is the command to do so:

```
ansible-playbook -i inventory.txt apache.yml
```

This command tells Ansible to use the inventory.txt file we created earlier as the inventory and to run the apache.yml playbook. Ansible will then connect to each node, gather facts, and execute the tasks defined in the playbook.

If everything is set up correctly, Ansible will install Apache on all your nodes. If Apache is already installed, Ansible will recognize this and skip the task.

The above program demonstrates the core concepts of Ansible and you can continue to explore more complex tasks, using variables and roles, and managing more than just package installations.

Trying out Complex Automation

To further explore Ansible's capabilities, let us create a more complex playbook. This playbook will install and configure Apache to serve a simple HTML page.

Below is what we want our playbook to do:

- Install Apache (as before)

- Create an HTML file on the server

- Modify the Apache configuration to serve this file

- Restart Apache so the changes take effect

Below is the playbook:

```yaml
- hosts: all
  become: yes
  tasks:
    - name: Ensure Apache is installed
      package:
        name: httpd
        state: present

    - name: Create a simple HTML file
      copy:
        content: "<h1>Welcome to our server!</h1>"
        dest: /var/www/html/index.html

    - name: Ensure Apache serves our HTML file
```

```yaml
  blockinfile:
    path: /etc/httpd/conf/httpd.conf
    block: |
      <Directory "/var/www/html">
        Options Indexes FollowSymLinks
        AllowOverride None
        Require all granted
      </Directory>
      DocumentRoot "/var/www/html"

- name: Ensure Apache is running and enabled at boot
  service:
    name: httpd
    state: started
    enabled: yes
```

Below is what each new task does:

- The copy module creates a file at the specified dest path. The file's content is the value of the content parameter.

- The blockinfile module inserts a block of text into a file. In this case, it's modifying the Apache configuration file to serve our HTML file.

- The service module ensures a service is running and enabled to start at boot. In this case, it's making sure Apache is running and will start automatically if the server reboots.

To run this playbook, use the same command as before:

```
ansible-playbook -i inventory.txt apache.yml
```

Now if you navigate to your nodes' IP addresses in a web browser, you should see "Welcome to our server!".

This playbook demonstrates Ansible's power to automate complex tasks. You can continue to add tasks to this playbook to further configure your servers, install additional software, or perform other administrative tasks.

Using Playbook to Configure Servers

To configure servers using the playbook, you need to target them in the inventory file. The inventory file is where you list all the servers (or "nodes") you want to manage with Ansible.

Below is a simple example of an inventory file:

```
[webservers]
192.0.2.1
192.0.2.2
```

In the above code snippet, webservers is a group that contains two nodes, identified by their IP addresses. You can also use hostnames if you prefer.

Now, update the hosts line in your playbook to target the webservers group:

```
- hosts: webservers
  become: yes
  tasks:
    # ...
```

With these changes, Ansible will run the playbook on all nodes in the webservers group when you use the ansible-playbook command:

```
ansible-playbook -i inventory.txt playbook.yml
```

In this case, inventory.txt is the name of your inventory file, and playbook.yml is the name of your playbook file.

When you run this command, Ansible will connect to each node in the webservers group, perform the tasks defined in your playbook, and report the results. Remember, to connect to your nodes, Ansible needs appropriate SSH credentials. You can provide these by adding a remote_user and ansible_ssh_private_key_file to your inventory file, or by running Ansible from a user that has passwordless SSH access to your nodes. If you're using a user with sudo privileges (as indicated by become: yes in the playbook), Ansible will also need the sudo password. You can provide this with the --ask-become-pass or -K option when you run ansible-playbook.

Remember to replace the IPs with your actual server IPs and update the tasks according to your configuration needs. You can include multiple groups and nodes in the inventory file to manage a large number of servers. Also, make sure to use the correct file paths and names according to your setup.

Using Ansible for Managing Softwares

You can use Ansible playbooks to manage software packages on your servers with the package management modules. Ansible has a module for most package managers on most Unix-like systems, including apt, yum, dnf, pkgng, etc. For our example, let us assume you are using a system with apt package manager, like Ubuntu.

The given below is a simple playbook that installs the nginx web server on all your web servers:

```
- hosts: webservers
  become: yes
  tasks:
    - name: Update apt cache
      apt:
        update_cache: yes

    - name: Install nginx
      apt:
        name: nginx
        state: present
```

Below is what this playbook does:

- The hosts: webservers line specifies that the playbook should run on all nodes in the webservers group.

- The become: yes line tells Ansible to use sudo to execute the tasks. This is necessary because package management typically requires root privileges.

- The tasks: line is followed by a list of tasks. Each task has a name that describes what it does, which is optional but recommended for readability.

- The apt: line indicates that this task uses the apt module.

- The update_cache: yes line tells the apt module to update the apt package cache before doing anything else. This is equivalent to running sudo apt update on the command line.

- The name: nginx line specifies that the apt module should manage the nginx package.

- The state: present line tells the apt module to ensure that nginx is installed. If nginx is not installed, the apt module will install it. If nginx is already installed, the apt module will do nothing.

You can run this playbook with the ansible-playbook command, just like before:

```
ansible-playbook -i inventory.txt playbook.yml
```

This command will install nginx on all nodes in the webservers group. If nginx is already installed, Ansible will ensure it's the latest version. If you want to install a specific version of a package, you can specify it using the = operator, e.g., name: nginx=1.14.0-0ubuntu1. Remember to replace the package name (nginx in the example) with the software you want to install.

Summary

In this chapter, we delved into Ansible, a popular open-source software tool for configuration management and automation. As a declarative IT automation platform, Ansible communicates with managed nodes and eliminates the need for dedicated remote systems. Built on Python, it uses YAML to express reusable descriptions of systems, making it versatile and straightforward to use, especially in network automation scenarios. We walked through the process of installing Ansible and setting it up in a Python environment, preparing the groundwork for more advanced operations.

We explored core Ansible concepts such as modules, tasks, and playbooks. Modules are units of code that Ansible executes, each designed for specific tasks. Tasks, on the other hand, are units of action in Ansible, while playbooks are the files where Ansible code is written. Playbooks, written in YAML, are human-readable, enabling easy orchestration of a multi-tier IT environment. We saw how to define and orchestrate simple automation using these concepts, providing a solid foundation for managing complex network configurations.

Finally, we used our knowledge of Ansible to execute more advanced operations, including server configuration and software installation using playbooks. By creating a playbook, we instructed Ansible to perform several tasks, including package updates and installation of new software on the target servers. This demonstrated Ansible's potential for simplifying and automating repetitive system administration tasks, freeing up resources for more strategic initiatives. Overall, Ansible's combination of simplicity, power, and wide community support makes it an excellent choice for network automation tasks.

Thank You

Index

Epilogue

Congratulations on completing "Python Networking 101"! You have now acquired the knowledge and skills required to excel as a network administrator using Python. Throughout this book, you have learned about various networking tasks, Python libraries, and best practices that will enable you to design, implement, and maintain efficient networks. As you begin your journey as a network administrator, it is important to remember that the world of networking is constantly evolving. New technologies, best practices, and tools are continually being developed, making it crucial for you to stay informed and up-to-date. By keeping yourself aware of the latest advancements, you will be able to adapt and grow in your career as a network administrator.

The skills you have gained in this book, combined with your dedication to continuous learning, will ensure that you are well-equipped to handle the challenges that come your way in the world of networking. As you progress, you may also consider diving deeper into specialized areas of networking, such as cloud networking, software-defined networking (SDN), or network security. Each of these areas offers unique opportunities for growth and specialization.

We hope that "Python Networking 101" has provided you with a solid foundation and the confidence to tackle networking tasks using Python. As you continue to practice and refine your skills, you will find that Python's versatility and extensive library ecosystem make it an indispensable tool for network administration. In addition to the practical skills you have gained, remember that networking is also about building connections with people. Collaborate with your peers, share your knowledge, and engage with the networking community to expand your horizons and further your growth.

Thank you for choosing "Python Networking 101" as your guide on this exciting journey. We wish you the best of luck in your future endeavors as a skilled network administrator, and we hope that you will continue to explore, learn, and grow in the ever-evolving world of networking.

Made in the USA
Monee, IL
07 July 2026

56549922R00105